Advance Praise for ALL WE WANT

"No writer is as humane, insightful, and clear-eyed as Michael Harris. His journey into the rabbit hole of consumer desire is one we all need to follow, and he makes it a joy along the way."
—Susan Orlean, author of *The Library Book*
and *The Orchid Thief*

"A feast of ideas, encounters, and brave exploration lovingly rendered." —John Vaillant, author of *The Golden Spruce*
and *The Jaguar's Children*

"After first chronicling many of the often-overlooked environmental and personal consequences of our grasping culture, *All We Want* goes on to propose a solution so humane and original, so possible, that it stands a chance of rescuing both our planet and our small, struggling selves. This is a marvellous, uplifting book, unique among others of its kind."
—Barbara Gowdy, author of *The White Bone* and *Little Sister*

"A gorgeous bit of magic is woven before our eyes. The prison humanity has built for itself—this sparkling maze of more—is transformed into an escape hatch. A damning study of humanity's insatiable appetites becomes a love song for our higher purpose."
—Arno Kopecky, author of *The Environmentalist's Dilemma*

"*All We Want* is a thoughtful examination of consumer desire, but it's much more than that. Harris's storytelling is entertaining, poignant, and totally eye-opening—a search for antidotes in our times of planetary emergency."
—Charlotte Gill, author of *Eating Dirt*

"A potent antidote to the culture of consumption destroying our planet from a philosopher-poet for our times. Harris offers inspiration and alternatives that could change the world."
—Carol Shaben, author of *Into the Abyss* and *The Marriott Cell*

"Desire, need, and what makes a good life. This eloquent treatise encourages us to rethink these timeless subjects, and to make our aperture of understanding both bigger and smaller— to appreciate both the sublime wonder of the world and the intimate acts of craft and care that contemporary capitalism obscures and devalues. This lyrical meditation is for everyone who feels trapped in the knowledge that our culture of consumer abundance depletes and destroys the environment without truly nourishing or satisfying our souls."
—Astra Taylor, author of *Remake the World*

"Michael Harris teaches us an essential lesson in a moving, beautifully written book. We pursue material things that wreck the planet and make us miserable while neglecting things that will make us happier and the world better. Worse yet, the more materialist we are, the more the things that matter recede from view. Time is running out. Reading this book may inspire you to blaze a more enlightened trail—to save yourself, those you love, and the earth."
—Barry Schwartz, author of *Why We Work* and co-author of *Practical Wisdom*

"We all know we need to trade our troubled relationship with consumerism for something more deeply satisfying and environmentally sane. Michael Harris does the hard work of understanding what that 'something' is, and shares the secret in flat-out dazzling writing full of wisdom and surprises."
—J.B. MacKinnon, author of *The Day the World Stops Shopping*

ALL

WE

WANT

ALSO BY MICHAEL HARRIS

*The End of Absence: Reclaiming What
We've Lost in a World of Constant
Connection*

*Solitude: In Pursuit of a Singular Life
in a Crowded World*

ALL WE WANT

Building the Life We Cannot Buy

MICHAEL HARRIS

DOUBLEDAY CANADA

Doubleday Canada and colophon are registered trademarks of Penguin Random House Canada Limited.

Poetry selection titled "World of the Future, We Thirsted" is from *Cast Away* by Naomi Shihab Nye. Copyright © 2020 by Naomi Shihab Nye. Used by permission of HarperCollins Publishers.

Library and Archives Canada Cataloguing in Publication

Title: All we want : building the life we cannot buy / Michael Harris.
Names: Harris, Michael, 1980- author.
Identifiers: Canadiana (print) 20210278226 | Canadiana (ebook) 20210278269 |
    ISBN 9780385695206 (hardcover) | ISBN 9780385695213 (EPUB)
Subjects: LCSH: Consumption (Economics) | LCSH: Consumption
    (Economics)—Moral and ethical aspects. | LCSH: Consumption
    (Economics)—Social aspects.
Classification: LCC HC79.C6 H37 2021 | DDC 306.3—dc23

Cover design: Kate Sinclair
Cover images: (front) CSA-Printstock, (back) Katsumi Muroushi;
both Getty Images

Printed in Canada

Published in Canada by Doubleday Canada, a division of
Penguin Random House Canada Limited

www.penguinrandomhouse.ca

10 9 8 7 6 5 4 3 2 1

Penguin
Random House
DOUBLEDAY CANADA

For my parents, Bob and Marilyn

CONTENTS

Gatsby believed in the green light, the orgiastic future
that year by year recedes before us. It eluded us then,
but that's no matter—tomorrow we will run faster,
stretch out our arms farther.

F. SCOTT FITZGERALD,
The Great Gatsby (1925)

Stripped of a sense of well-being,
we downed our water from small disposable bottles.
Casting the plastic to streetside,
we poured high-potency energy tonics or Coke
down our throats, because this time in history
had sapped us so thoroughly and
we were desperate....

NAOMI SHIHAB NYE,
"World of the Future, We Thirsted" (2020)

PART I

The Story

1

A PRETTY HILL

WE'D BEEN DRIVING for several hours when we decided to pull off the highway and watch the world burn. Having passed the town of Hope, and climbed the Coquihalla Summit, my husband and I were now well into the wooded mountains of central British Columbia, and so had a view of the disaster. Above, the sun glowed scarlet through a perpetual haze of smoke. The sky was a wash of copper and bourbon, as it had been for most of that summer. Through miles of obscuring soot we could see thick columns of fresh grey where today's fires were burning. We had heard on the radio that more than a million hectares of forest would be lost.

At the rest stop there was a Dairy Queen, sitting alone on a cement promontory, contained and proud as a temple. The air in its parking lot was not breathable and so we went inside, where we met a uniformed young man who seemed surprised to have any company.

We bought two ice creams and stood at the window, observing the apocalypse as we ate. It had been many years since I'd eaten Dairy Queen ice cream and I revelled in its sickly sweetness. Minutes later we threw out our plastic spoons and cups and spoiled napkins. Sated, we walked back to the car and, between the Dairy Queen's entrance and the door of our Honda Civic, I noticed dark dots of something flying into my glasses, onto my T-shirt. I looked up, into the bruised sky, and saw billions of black flecks swarming toward us. Ash was raining down.

THIS WAS A couple seasons ago. We have since learned to pack masks and also to check the fire report before travelling in summer.

Looking back at that moment, it does seem like an omen. The world scorched while we blithely ate our ice cream. And if we could ignore that omen, it was only because omens had grown so commonplace. Glaciers melted and calved; the planet's biodiversity collapsed. Epic variations on a single theme: the material world was trembling with coming change. The status quo was cracking against the limits of real life.

I didn't know it yet, but there were other omens coming. A pandemic was coming for everyone. A separate catastrophe was coming for my family. And everywhere there hovered a premonition that life, as it had been laid out for us, was insupportable.

Meanwhile, we ate our ice cream. Ordinary days proceeded, requiring a cognitive dissonance, a willful blindness to the emergency at hand. Slowly, though, an awareness of this hypocrisy built up in my mind. I would debate with my husband the uselessness of trying to change (and then its necessity); I'd read an article and look up to find every item in our home radiating with its own toxic cost; and all these moments slipped over my vision like successive lenses, slowly bringing things into focus. Finally it couldn't be denied: the consumer culture surrounding me was a feeble kind of artifice, a simplistic story—and that story was ending.

Still, like most, I held on to the dream I'd been given, the dream of consumer happiness. It was shining still on television, in magazines, and in every luxurious household I entered. I held on to this dream even as it grew preposterous and obscene.

The consumer story hung around me, as it hung around everyone I knew. It coloured what we saw, infected every breath, and usually felt like a natural, everlasting part of the world. Some stories are like that—they draw us in to a fabricated forever-moment, suspend us outside the torrent of real history.

Abandoning the consumer story, finding some new mode of being, seemed as crucial as it was unlikely. But I decided to make a beginning, at least. And I decided that beginning would be where consumption ends: the landfill.

I'D NEVER BEEN before, never had a reason. Landfills hold what we want to forget. But maybe there was another explanation for my avoidance: landfills hold what we want forgiven.

Things used, things broken, things lost both with regret and without. To pause a moment and tally all we toss is to register the expenses that undergird our precious consumer culture—it is to look at what we have and all we enjoy as an unsustainable spree, an untenable little tale.

On arrival at Vancouver's landfill, I met a woman called Lynn, my City-appointed guide. She was friendly and no-nonsense in steel-toed boots and a reflective safety vest. I liked her, liked how proud she was of the landfill's work.

We climbed a hill of garbage. I could see bits of metal, cables, chairs, bottles, bags of whatever should or shouldn't be there. All the things my city had wanted once but wanted no more. A monster truck cruised over it all—each steel-studded tire weighing more than seven thousand pounds—stamping and squashing the garbage into the shape of a gentle hill. Once the driver was satisfied with his mound, the garbage would be given a plastic cap and topped with soil and grass seed. It would be turned into an idea of nature, a sweet hill with asbestos running through it in a vein of fibrous silver.

At the hill's crest I met a dun-coloured eagle. A juvenile, I supposed. It was busy sorting through scraps of rotten food and tangles of plastic. Eventually the bird tired, or else had its fill of apple cores and shopping bags. With a great heave it went skyward and then down again, perching on a fencepost ten feet from my face. The creature ignored me and stared back at the expanse of junk. To its left, on the next post, another eagle stood; and there was another on the post after that. Soon I realized there were hundreds of eagles standing sentry on that fence, circling a portion of the landfill, their scavenger stares meeting at the heap where my city's freshest trash had been piled. I studied them a while but at last followed their collective gaze back toward the promising field of garbage. We were like stone gargoyles then, the eagles and I, staring inward at the place where a cathedral ought to be.

Turning, I saw how the whole landfill was made of more rolling hills—225 hectares of them in all. You could fit the country of Monaco inside. Strangely, there were flowers on the pretend hills, too. Happy little dots of orange and blue. At the lush perimeter, a deer was grazing. The clouds of seagulls you'd expect at a dump had been erased: a falconer came each day with his raptors to scare them off. (Only the eagles were undeterred.) I had to admit it was all very pretty, would even be peaceful were it not for the procession of burping trucks. Pretty as a movie set.

Lynn blushed, though, when I asked about a recent fire that raged for nineteen days inside one of those hills. When smoke had slithered out, workers excavated to inspect—flooding the anaerobic environment below with oxygen and turning what had only been a smoulder into a full, raging flame. Every landfill is, by its nature, a kind of suppressed threat.

Lynn and I came down the hill and passed a lot crowded with car-sized metal boxes—clothing-donation bins that used to be stationed all over the city. "That's weird," I offered, pointing.

"Yes," she said, "we have a lot of those, because of the issues." Later, I remembered the bins were banned after five people died inside of them. (I'd thought the victims were trapped while digging for old shirts and pants, but a cop informed me

they'd climbed in looking for a soft place to rest while inject-
ing drugs.)

Landfills are acquainted with our deepest shame. A few
years ago, thirty police in hazard suits dug through those
pretty hills for days before they found the remains of a new-
born baby boy. His mother, having given birth in her boy-
friend's bathroom, had wrapped the child in a towel and
placed him in a garbage bin at a nearby school. It is unknown
whether the child was stillborn or not.

I wondered what, if anything, the landfill had *not* taken
into itself. Watching the every-colour pile of goods being
shaped into that smooth and blameless hill, watching workers
prepare to cover it all with an obliterating skin of soil, I mar-
velled at the sheer multitudes such places must contain.

VANCOUVER'S LANDFILL IS not so significant a lump—it's
only a microcosm, a sampling of the world's wastage. Round
up all we toss and the mind reels: we produce more than two
billion tonnes of garbage every year (our children's generation is expected to produce 3.4 billion tonnes).[1] About fifty
million tonnes of that is "e-waste"—all the TVs and phones,
the printers and tablets, the useless fax machine from your
grandfather's basement, the ransomware-addled iMac from
your mother's den.[2] And no longer is our trash limited to the
Earth; while our ancestors could only bury their leftovers in
three feet of dirt, we rocket ours to the stars, filling the heavens with refuse. The moon hosts 400,000 pounds of garbage
already, including ninety-six bags of astronaut urine, feces,

and vomit.[3] Half a million pieces of "space junk" are whipping around the planet, too, travelling at seventeen thousand miles per hour to nowhere at all.[4]

Even my hometown landfill is so swollen it will take no more after 2036. When I asked Lynn where the new site would be she blinked and said, "No—no plans yet."

"But it's going to be full soon. Where will all our stuff go?" That year alone, 721,000 tonnes of waste were brought there and many tonnes more were shipped south to America.[5]

A shrug. "They haven't figured that out."

A little while later, when my visit was winding down, Lynn said, "I try to keep all this as unnoticed and pleasant as possible." She gestured at the pretty hill past the line of trucks. "I'm the one who planted those flowers."

2

UNTENABLE

EIGHTY MILLION YEARS ago an ocean called the Tethys stretched between unrecognizable continents—a forgotten ocean lapping at forgotten shores. The Earth was bluer then, with water covering four-fifths of its surface. Shorelines swelled hundreds of metres higher than today's. Tyrannosaurus rex stalked her prey on land but the real drama, for our purposes, was in the water.

At the sun-spangled surface of the Tethys a bonanza of life was possible. Fuelled by the steady warmth of the Cretaceous climate, blooms of plankton thrived—zooplankton of wormy or squid-like form gobbled their photosynthesizing cousins, the phytoplankton. Mostly, they were all too small to be noticed, even had a human been around to take a look. (A million lives may be suspended in a single drop of seawater.) Their numbers were so vast, however, so unaccountably vast, that an observer in outer space, looking down on this blue planet, would have wondered at their cloudy, aggregate immensity.

Eighty million years ago these swarms multiplied through-out the waves of the Tethys, lived their microscopic lives—only a few days each—and died. Then, in motes of marine snow, the spent plankton fell through the ocean's blind depths, each speck smuggling an infinitesimal parcel of the sun's energy downward. Over weeks of drifting descent most of the plankton were eaten by larger animals, and what did touch down was mostly eaten by creatures that cruised the ocean floor. But perhaps one percent of all the plankton was spared and buried by sediment. Over time, the sediment piled up, grain by grain, and once the covering reached two or three kilometres in height the furnace at the planet's core could warm those trillions of buried bodies until they broke down into hydrocarbons. This seepage became the oil that would fuel our world. And prepared in its shifting darkness was something more, as well—a story about life, a story that waited tens of millions of years to be read by us.

Why do I find the image of marine snow so compelling, so incantatory? It is, in one sense, the most ordinary scene imaginable. Life lived, life spent—life tumbling forever into sunless depths. Marine snow is quotidian. And yet, over the course of vast eons, it becomes also extraordinary—because the possibility of our entire consumer culture is the result. Imagine those years, stretched out by the millions, by the tens of millions; imagine the thrumming heat of our planet, the miracle of this universe's physics; imagine it all conspiring to give us such a splurge of incalculable wealth. Imagine thinking all that wealth was history's goal.

You were made to consume, says the story. *This is your purpose and meaning.*

To meditate on the planet's work—to see the marine snow trail down in its darkening clouds and connect that to a false hill stuffed with thrown-away things, is to comprehend the obscene cost of not just oil production but the whole entrenched getting-and-spending narrative we've been humming to ourselves for centuries.

AND YET. We live in a moment where we may imagine new narratives. Indeed, they're thrust upon us. Compared to where their parents stood at forty, millennials in the West have lower incomes, higher debts, and virtually no wealth to fall back on. They have an average net worth of less than $8,000, making them the worst-off generation in modern history.[6] The even-younger members of Generation Z have similarly dashed hopes.[7] Meanwhile, work lives are fragile and uncertain. Marriage, home ownership, and children are all delayed. If the young ever retire at all, it's likely to be in their mid-seventies—which will be cold comfort in the US,[8] England,[9] and other nations where life expectancies have been dropping or plateauing. But, in all this, there's a useful disillusionment. The young have seen the stress and cracks in our story of forever growth.

My point is not that material culture completely failed today's youth; in the developed world, in fact, they own twice as many things as their grandparents did.[10] Neither do I mean that millennial angst about RRSPs and bankrupt social security nets is likely to upend a consumer culture centuries in the making. The point is that the dream of the twentieth century has been shaken by ecological, economic, and even viral disaster; so much so that we have an opportunity to notice its fabricated, fantastical nature. Millennials are entering their forties during the 2020s having known regular disappointments and derailments, recessions and reversals, yearly admonishments that life is not, after all, some bonanza laid out for their pleasure; and so they're alive to the absurd contradictions at the heart of the tale they were told about material comforts and consumer bliss. The larger promises of "the good life"—job stability, real estate, and comfortable retirement—all failed to materialize. In fact, my generation will be the last to read that shining, unadulterated fantasy about consumerism and the first to scan the shelves, asking what comes next. We have noticed that the old story is absurd and nostalgic. We have noticed that, as true as the consumer story felt in the twentieth century, it has run aground on the realities of the twenty-first.

We notice the crisis but hesitate at the brink of change. Five trillion plastic bags like the one I watched that eagle gobble are still used every year to tote home our athleisure outfits and Cheerios.[11] In rich countries like America we toss sofas and rugs as easily as coffee cups. A lifestyle that would, to our ancestors, have appeared obscenely decadent appears middling to us. And this consumer lifestyle of insatiable want is adopted by millions more each year as developing nations join our entwined marketplace. By 2030 the global middle class (those able to not just cover the basics but spend a little extra on whatever they like) is expected to reach 5.6 billion (a growth of two billion in just a decade) and those new customers will not be angels, abstaining from the spoils on offer;[12] they will, as ecologist William Rees puts it, be "pounding on the door to be let in [to our] energy-addicted consumer party."[13] This is, in fact, the plan. China, for example, is no longer content to be the "factory of the world"; it sees domestic consumer growth as crucial in an uncertain future with rocky trade relations; this means making its workers into shoppers.[14]

Of course, if the goal is only to lift the world to American standards, and not to reduce the standards of Americans, it would mean each of us dumping twenty tonnes of CO_2 into the atmosphere every year—a quadrupling of the global average.[15] It's commonplace to say a world full of Americans would need four or five planets to support all those well-fed citizens. But the absurdity of that image, planet stacked upon planet— a vision as wrongheaded as a medieval map of the heavens— should remind us what *untenable* really means.

It took several thousand years to consume our first trillion barrels of oil, but we will guzzle the next trillion in thirty years alone—a geological instant compared to the millions of years it took to create it. One expert told me there's perhaps a century's worth of accessible oil left, "being quite generous,"[16] and BP reports there are only proven reserves to last us half that time.[17] Even if we solve "the oil problem" tomorrow, and pivot toward alternative forms of energy, we will still have to look over the clear-cuts, the stripped mines, the poisoned oceans, and reckon with a far larger existential dilemma: *What will keep us from eating the world?* We seem programmed to burn it up, toss it away—if not by our nature exactly, then by the corporate hands that manipulate our nature so well.

This finale is such a hum of consumption that the planet itself is warmed. I write these words during the hottest year on record—and the hottest decade. (The most glaring, too. We bleach the night sky two percent brighter every year.[18]) Those enormous swarms of plankton that covered the Tethys are reincarnated as toxic blue-green algae blooms larger than the island of Manhattan; the algae thrives in warmed-up waters and kills off the millions of animals it poisons.[19] Such catastrophes are daily news, though. I only need to glance at the latest press releases to find that warming temperatures have severed from the western edge of Antarctica an iceberg the size of Malta—three hundred square kilometres. The hottest day ever recorded there—18.3 degrees Celsius—has just occurred.[20] (It was the same temperature in Los Angeles that day.) New studies find rising sea levels will displace at least 190 million people by the end of this century, and perhaps more than 600 million.[21] As I write, a cataclysmic period of drought and fire has engulfed Australia, incinerating sixteen million acres[22] before easing into a season of floods with two feet of water rushing over baked earth[23]—a case of what specialists call "compound extremes."[24] As many as a billion animals were killed by those fires, including photogenic koalas, wallabies, and kangaroos, but also less popular species of rodent, reptile, and frog, whose devastation went barely noticed.

None of this is a surprise or aberration. We are living through the Holocene extinction event, which will see human activity end roughly one million species over the next few decades.[25] Since 1962, when Rachel Carson published *Silent Spring*, three billion birds have already vanished from the skies of North America.[26] More than a quarter of all the continent's birds, gone: half the meadowlarks and northern bobwhites; a third of the sanderlings and plovers; fifty million sparrows; fifty million finches; fifty million blackbirds; the swallows and thrushes and starlings, too, all rubbed from the sky by the millions, great empty blue left behind. Blank as the air above that landfill I visited. They told me a falconer scared away the gulls but maybe all those missing birds were just that—missing. Only the eagles—powerful, ruthless, privileged—left alive to scavenge among the scraps.

WE WERE, of course, warned.

In 1972 a team of MIT researchers published a groundbreaking report titled *The Limits to Growth*, which used a new computer model to predict that by 2072 we will run up against the fact of finite resources and face "sudden and uncontrollable decline in both population and industrial capacity."[27] Our expansionist culture would, in a century, be scraping the bottom of the capitalist barrel. There was nothing so very novel about the report's findings. Even Aristotle noted that societies, like plants and animals, should grow to a mature size and then enjoy a period of stasis. (When things continue to grow unchecked, we don't call that "thriving," we call it cancer.) What was new about the *Limits* report was the exacting authority of its authors—a team representing more than a dozen experts from various fields—and the enormous scope of their data.

Here was a global and far-sighted assessment of long-term trends in world population, industrialization, pollution, food production, and the depletion of resources, all laid out with an unprecedented level of granularity. And a simple, ruthless reality came into focus: if we failed to dramatically limit ourselves, things would be limited on our behalf—in the form of a planet-wide cataclysm. A sustainable future, in which all people have their basic needs met and civilization as we know it basically continues, was certainly possible; but every passing year without radical transformation made this happier outcome less feasible. If we failed to self-impose limits, if we surpassed the carrying capacity of the planet, numbers would be balanced on our behalf by widespread famine and industrial collapse. Avoiding that catastrophe meant lowering birth rates to match our death rates; diverting capital away from the production of material goods; cutting the average income in wealthy countries like America in half (while tripling the incomes of the average global citizen); and massively restricting resource consumption. The authors of *Limits* acknowledged that "there is almost no historical precedent for such an approach,"[28] and that the kind of wholesale societal change they were calling for, a shift toward de-growth, seemed next to impossible; it would "tax the ingenuity, the flexibility, and the self-discipline of the human race."[29] They would not have proposed such changes at all were it not for the calamitous consequences of inaction.

Many ridiculed the report: it was too simplistic, did not allow for marvellous technological advances that would save the day; its Malthusian fatalism was the stuff of cranks who

couldn't fathom a "dematerialized" economy that would proceed without natural resources. Oxford economist Wilfred
Beckerman spoke for those who rejected a hamstrung future,
saying: "If growth were to be abandoned as an objective of
policy, democracy too would have to be abandoned. Whatever the 'costs of growth' in terms of the quality of the environment—[and] these costs are probably negligible—the costs
of deliberate non-growth, in terms of the political and social
transformation that would be required in society, are astro-
nomical."[30] The *Limits* team began to look far more prescient,
though, in the twenty-first century. Writing at the turn of the
millennium, economist (and George W. Bush energy advisor)
Matthew Simmons admitted, "In hindsight, [they] turned out
to be right. We simply wasted thirty years ignoring this work."[31]

I SOUGHT OUT Jørgen Randers, a co-author of the *Limits*
report. He was at his home in Norway, just coming inside after
a barbecue with family. His brow furrowed, his hair slicked
and silver. "I was left with all the mess," he grumbled.

Randers spent decades arguing for de-growth in the midst
of the plentiful and prosperous twentieth century. He had little
patience now. What followed was a long chat—part conversation, part lecture. Randers, now seventy-four, required little in
the way of questions, often preferring to turn the tables and
question me, instead. (*What is your age and level of education?
By the sound of your voice, you're of Irish descent?*) I seemed to
be a point of demographic data, something Randers was compelled to assess before we could proceed. At last, however, we
did proceed, and I asked him about the fallout of his report.

Decades, he told me, "of totally futile discussion." *Limits* was no doomsday prophecy—it did not promise that humanity was coming to an end. But it did cause an uproar because of the simple—and yet audacious—claim that continuous growth on a finite planet is liable to run into an arithmetic problem. The report caught the attention (and ire) of the world's macroeconomists—princes of the social sciences—who felt it was treading on their turf. Randers and his team were focused on the limits of the physical world, things like population size and oil reserves, but the macroeconomists feared they were making a strong argument against the perpetual growth of Gross Domestic Product, and that was a limit too far. They therefore went to war, claiming *Limits* was bunk, and even demanding that MIT, which employed *Limits'* authors, expel the traitors from its ranks. At the same time, leaders in the developing world saw the report as a message from rich white men who didn't want poor nations to get a slice of the consumer pie. (From their perspective, growth was necessary in order to escape poverty; a limit on growth was a limit on life.) Tormented first by critics and then by lethargic bureaucracies, Randers saw his message obstructed and misconstrued, ignored and warped. And so I asked him, almost half a century later, to state his thesis as simply as he could.

"Can the ecological footprint of man grow forever on a finite planet? We would say absolutely no. And we illustrate one other thing."

"What's that?"

"If we try to expand our footprint, our resource use, pollution, if we try to push all that beyond the carrying capacity of the planet, we will succeed for a while. Thirty years or so. And then we will be forced back by Mother Nature." I imagined a meniscus of water trembling above the rim of a glass, a tenuous extension before collapse.

Randers is not a fatalist. Folded into his belief in numbers is a belief, however small, that change is possible, that our future is nothing but a product of present inputs. And so he advocates for one overarching change: we must now value our well-being more than GDP and consumption. He's devised a "well-being index," in fact, which he and his colleagues use to judge whether a country is supporting the needs of the working majority. There are five components: after-tax income; government spending per person; income equity; environmental quality; and hope.[32]

"Hope?" I asked. "What does hope mean?"

"Hope," he said, "is the inverse of climate change. The more the temperature warms, the lower is the hope for a peaceful and pleasant life for our children and grandchildren."

Randers's well-being index may appear self-explanatory— of course a clean, equitable, hopeful future is a worthy aim—but much of our common struggle remains directed elsewhere, toward the expansion of GDP. Despite polls showing most people (especially in times of crisis) wish their governments focused on quality of life and well-being, it is "growth" that remains the obsession of policy-makers.[33] This "growth" so beloved by the macroeconomists and so often touted by politicians as proof of happy days may, in fact, take place without any rewards flowing to the poor or the middle classes. A country's GDP can look very healthy on paper while a few oligarchs reap the lion's share of wealth. "Per capita GDP in the United States of America has doubled since 1970," Randers noted, "but the rich have taken the whole benefit of economic development."

How much faith did he have, I wondered? Was humanity doomed to expire in a landfill of its own making? Randers was on record supporting the famous activist Greta Thunberg, for example, whose strike mobilized people in 150 countries to demand action on climate change. I marched in one of those protests myself, saw my seven-year-old nephew there lugging a placard. But demanding action and creating it are not the same. There have been many climate agreements in recent decades (aside from Paris, there was the Kyoto Protocol, the Copenhagen Accord) but CO_2 concentration in the atmosphere has not been checked. In fact, it reached its highest point in human history, 415 parts per million, in 2020—48 percent higher than pre-industrial levels. (The last time CO_2 levels were this high was three million years ago, when oceans were 15–25 metres higher.)[34] "I must admit," began Randers, "that in my heart . . ." He did not complete the thought, saying instead, "I saw the youth rise when *I* was a youth, in the nineteen-seventies; we started Earth Day. Then I saw it again in the nineteen-nineties when the Nature Conservation Movement grew. And now it comes again . . ."

I thought about how it must feel to be crying out for change, to champion change over decades while seeing the most corrosive of human stories—this tale of consumption and resource hoarding—win every time. How would it feel to prophesy what one knows to be true for a heedless public; how would it feel to be so recklessly ignored like some Cassandra? Even if Greta Thunberg's generation is galvanized for meaningful change, even if they vote in progressive leaders who take action in the decades to come, Randers seemed disappointed in humanity as a whole, in our short-sighted adherence to the one, tired tale.

He took a breath and the rattle reminded me I was speaking to a man too old to ever see the future he'd predicted. "Let me say, I desperately hope that the young of today really understand they are destroying their own future."

I BEGAN ASKING friends what they thought GDP was. Answers included:

"It's how good the economy is."

"It's how wealthy we are."

"It's the country's overall welfare."

In fact, Gross Domestic Product is simply the total monetary value of all goods and services a nation produces in a given year. If GDP increases, the economy is said to be expanding; if GDP decreases, the economy is said to be shrinking. The fact that this marker became the defining metric of the twentieth century, a stand-in for the health of a nation, is a testament to the consumer story's powerful grip. We have learned to define GDP growth as the *only* growth. But Simon Kuznets, the Nobel-winning economist who was the first to develop a set of national income accounts (for a US Congress report in 1937), explicitly noted it could not measure the country's well-being. In Kuznets's report he reminds Congress that, "the welfare of a nation can scarcely be inferred" by such a metric.[35] And, years later, he went further: "Distinctions must be kept in mind between quantity and quality of growth, between costs and returns, and between the short and long run . . . goals for 'more' growth should specify more growth of what and for what."[36] Kuznets lamented that, for example, a country can expand its GDP a great deal by simply militarizing. Not all growth is the same.

Global GDP is several times larger today than it was in the heart of the twentieth century, and this change is credited with lifting many out of extreme poverty in developing nations. However, as Randers noted, in wealthier countries like the United States a rising GDP no longer signifies a rising quality of life for the ordinary citizen. GDP has in many ways become a thermometer not of society's health but of a consumer culture that benefits the wealthy alone. And nowhere is this more obvious than when we see runaway consumption poisoning the planet on which we all depend. Failing to honour the Paris Agreement, for example, will line some pockets while sacrificing a million lives each year to air pollution alone.[37] And then the climate change exacerbated by our rocketing economies will, ironically, also *imperil* those economies down the line. In 2018, for example, even as the Trump administration worked tirelessly to remove environmental protections, thirteen US agencies released a joint report warning that climate change would cause the American GDP to shrink up to 10 percent by the end of the century.[38] (Again, we can expect limits imposed on us when they aren't freely chosen.) Meanwhile, hurricanes, intensified by climate change,[39] can now each cause more than $100 billion in damage. Heat waves put tens of thousands of people into hospital, adding a burden to strained systems. In my own country, a government-funded think tank predicts damage from climate change will cost Canada $21–$43 billion annually by 2050.[40] And the Economist Intelligence Unit predicts that fallout from warming temperatures will shrink the global economy, too.[41]

Many economists and politicians have doubled down, insisting that growth is the only path forward. They argue that we can keep expanding our economies without destroying the planet. We are promised that, thanks to technological advances, the growth game can go on while carbon emissions fall away. However, the Jevons Paradox (named for nineteenth-century economist William Stanley Jevons) points out that breakthroughs in resource efficiency are often cancelled out by an increase in consumer demand.[42] Use oil or copper or wood more efficiently and we simply up our idea of normal consumption, undoing any environmental benefit. (For example, as refrigerators became more energy-efficient, they doubled in size.) This paradox is playing out on a global scale: despite marvellous advances in efficiency, we are failing to honour the Paris Agreement which would cap global temperature increases at 1.5 or 2 degrees Celsius above pre-industrial levels. The United Nations reports that we're on track to produce about 50 percent more fossil fuels than would be consistent with a 2-degree-Celsius pathway—and 120 percent more than would be consistent with a 1.5-degree pathway.[43] So far, we are not inventing our way out of this catastrophe.

Renewable energy is of course hopeful, but it is only a fledgling and partial solution. Eighty-four percent of the world's energy is still derived from fossil fuels.[44, 45] And, as per the Jevons Paradox, the increase in demand for energy over the next few decades is expected to outpace all increases in renewables.[46] The Oxford economist Kate Raworth has warned that, despite the promise of green tech, our addiction to unending growth "cannot be decoupled from resource use on anything like the scale required to bring us safely back within planetary limits."[47]

Time and again, the plan to spin up a dematerialized future must be footnoted with some hidden, very material cost. Figures about what "goes into" the things we consume are often silent, for example, about the fossil fuels used to extract and transport materials. In fact, the twentieth century was one long experiment in making waste invisible; we cover our landfills with flowers. But each of us would walk home with an additional three hundred shopping bags of stuff each week if we had to carry all the material needed to make the things we consume.[48]

Even our digital products, which pretend to derive from something as insubstantial as "the cloud," are not blameless. Take a popular YouTube offering—the music video for the 2017 hit "Despacito," which was viewed five billion times in its first year: at that rate, the video consumed the same amount of energy as forty thousand American homes.[49, 50] Whenever we imagine we have slipped through the gate, beaten a material limit, an unexpected tax rises to meet us.

RANDERS PROMISED A tipping point after which de-growth is simply mandated by the constitution of the natural world.

He warned that larger laws will take over if humans fail to produce their own equilibrium. We'll be forced, then, to know a life without heedless sprees of consumption—forced to abandon the story we mistook for reality.

But ours is a disaster with a thread of hope—because, in abandoning the dominant story of the twentieth century, we may finally discover stories suited to the twenty-first. Shortly after winning the 2019 Nobel Memorial Prize in Economic Sciences, Abhijit Banerjee declared, "There are no iron laws of economics keeping us from building a more humane world."[51] And, as though to prove his claim, that same year New Zealand's government declared they would no longer use GDP as a guiding light; instead, the Happiness Index (which measures success by the well-being of citizens) would reign.[52] Money immediately flowed toward housing programs and victims of violence. The idea of forever growth, forever consumption, is a fiction that can—and must—be rewritten.

We saw the potential for change when six million protesters took to the streets in Thunberg's Climate Strike; we saw it again when COVID-19 shuttered the world. We are witnessing, in these pivotal moments, something unlikely and necessary—the start of different stories.

The world's population is expected to peak in the twenty-first century (somewhere between nine and eleven billion) and then, in an almost unfathomable reversal, our numbers will stall and even shrink.[53, 54] Will new technologies buoy up economies even as our population falls away? Perhaps. But we will still have to reckon with the existential math problem of infinite growth on a finite planet.

How much grace can we bring to bear as we re-envision what a virtuous, powerful, happy, meaningful life looks like in our own uncertain century? Since we are failing to stave off the worst of climate change, since overwhelming revisions and reversals are certain to dominate in the coming years, it seems vital to adopt new ways to measure our lives. Vital because the story we tell ourselves about what makes a life worth living is the animus, the hope and fuel, that gets us through.

New stories are coming. They can be told by us or by the hurricanes.

3

THE RAT WHO
WOULD NOT EAT

A CHEMISTRY OF want bubbles inside my head.

Show me a cue—a hamburger, a pile of cash, a beautiful home—and my resource-hungry midbrain releases the neurotransmitter dopamine. All that dopamine then carries its message of *want* down my mesolimbic pathway to the nucleus accumbens in my basal forebrain. And it's there that dopamine makes me conscious of the perceived importance of things, propelling me toward gluttonous behaviour: eat the burger, steal the cash, buy the . . . anything. Dopamine's job in this scenario is simple: maximize future resources, motivate me to overcome obstacles. Grab that Big Mac.

Describing the chemistry of consumption in this way, using words like *neurotransmitter* and *mesolimbic*, leaves me feeling both regretful and calm. Regretful because, like most people, I don't want to think of my impulse to buy as the work of mere chemicals. I want to be driven by something more than a drop of dopamine. And calm because, at the same time, this framework relieves me of responsibility for my otherwise indefensible desires. As much as I want to believe in my free will, I also want to believe that I can't do anything *but* consume as much as I do.

There is one daunting argument for such fatalism: humans have an extraordinary amount of dopamine at play compared to other animals, and researchers believe this is why our reach so wildly exceeds our grasp. Ravens are next in line when we rank dopamine levels (not orangutangs or dolphins) and this accounts for their industrious nature.[55] A raven who wants the food inside your trash can, for example, will patiently build a tool using a multi-step process in order to tip the can over. Their dopamine levels inspire a dogged—well, *ravenous*—want.

All animals have their own wants, of course—they want food, sex, shelter. They may even pursue these things with ferocity. But humans pine for the faraway, even the impossible; our hungers can be as abstract as they are insatiable.

It's dopamine that makes us love the story of consumer culture so well. It primes us to believe there's always some *resource*, some treasure, to collect next. It fuels a primal instinct to consume.

HOW DID DOPAMINE come to dominate us? Here's one theory:

Two million years ago, our ancestors were small and weak compared to other animals. Worse, their legs couldn't keep up with a galloping beast. These early hominids shouldn't have had much luck when hunting big game or searching for valuable carrion. And yet our ancestors had one singular advantage: an ability to profusely sweat—and, by sweating, regulate their temperature. While prey could easily outrun them at the outset, the chase could last for hours if need be, even in the midday sun of a bone-dry savannah. Eventually other animals were driven to a state of heat exhaustion and collapse, allowing our ancestors to simply jog up and make their kill. By allowing an extension of hunting and midday scavenging, sweat changed the game.[56]

All that sweating had another, unexpected consequence, though—for our dopamine levels. Dopamine has more than one job; while it's known for driving want, it moonlights as part of our cooling system. So, achieving rapid thermoregulation only became possible with an expanded dopaminergic system. This means that when our ancestors gained the ability to sweat buckets, they would have massively boosted their dopamine levels in the bargain.[57, 58] We began sweating so we could pursue resources with new levels of intensity—and the dopamine that made all that sweating possible amped up our drive in tandem. A new capacity for gathering resources led not to satiation but to greater want. (Unsurprisingly, it was around this time in our evolution we first made stone tools.) All this seems to be a chemical manifestation of the truth that our wants have a habit of growing to match new possibilities.

I discussed this one afternoon with Professor Daniel Z. Lieberman, who has devoted much of his career to studying dopamine. He sat in his office at George Washington University, beneath prints of tropical seascapes and a poster of his new book cover, which shows the human brain as a bouquet of flowers—the book's title is also his nickname for dopamine, *The Molecule of More*. Lieberman is a warm presence, toothy and friendly; he has a knack for combining a psychiatrist's curiosity with a professor's command. And as he spoke, the mechanics and evolutionary imperatives all made a certain fascinating sense. What didn't make sense (to me, at least) was how anyone could consider these drives well-adapted to modern life.

"Wait a minute," I interrupted. "The average American bought sixty-six pieces of clothing last year.[59] That's where this hunting drive took us. Why aren't the brakes getting pumped?"

"Oh, yes," he replied. "Most of us already have access to all the food and shelter and so on that we could ever need. So our dopamine systems sort of flail around for other things to get."

"Is the biology getting . . . hijacked by the culture?"

"Exactly that. There's a giant difference between the rate of change brought about by evolution in a biological organism and the rate of change in the availability of resources brought about by culture. You know, culture changes dramatically in a hundred years. Evolution not at all." Our dopamine system has not fundamentally changed in the last million years, in fact—one scientist later told me its roots may go back 600 million years, to a common dopaminergic ancestor we share with lobsters and beetles. So, from an evolutionary standpoint, we are still stuck in ancient times, in a world of resource scarcity, even while those of us in wealthy countries cruise gleaming aisles at overstocked grocery stores.

They say a goldfish will eat until its intestines rupture. There is no concept of "enough" bred into its DNA because at no point in its evolution was "enough" a meaningful factor. Many companies have discovered a similar glitch in human programming and focus on triggering dopamine circuits rather than improving the products being sold. It's far easier to manipulate my dopamine levels via flashing Instagram ads than to invest in expensive R&D.

Some of us are more susceptible to these traps than others. Some swim in dopamine and it becomes the guiding principle of their lives, pushing them to not just amass personal resources but to seek influence over the resources of others. In other words, some of us are politicians.

"You know Bill Clinton?" he asked.

"Sure."

"Obviously that guy has a lot of dopamine. To be president of the United States you've gotta be *sloshing around* in dopamine." Clinton, though, has a relatively steady brain, with dopamine circuits balanced by circuits associated with feelings of satisfaction—circuits dealing in endorphins, oxytocin, and serotonin. "People meet Bill Clinton and he seems like a good old boy," Lieberman said. "He has ethical shortcomings for sure but he's also the kind of guy you'd watch a football game with. That's a sign of high levels of things like serotonin balancing out the dopamine."

"And then somebody like Donald Trump?"

"Tonnes and tonnes and *tonnes* of dopamine. But it's much more imbalanced. You're not going to spend your Saturday afternoon with that guy."

Lieberman was quick to point out that we aren't always victims of our chemistry; we can work to rebalance our minds the same way an athlete rebalances her body by working out different muscle groups. An overly dopaminergic person may practice mindfulness, for example, to train themselves away from a state of constant want toward more contentment.

I am often stunned, nonetheless, by the opposite tendency: my ability to nurse avarice in the face of a climate crisis that should deter me. Like most people, I seem hard-wired to consume at levels that assure my own future misery—or at least the misery of future generations. Conversations at dinner swirl around new houses, new cars, and better-paying jobs as easily as they swirl around toxic oceans and inhumane factory conditions. This is cognitive dissonance as survival strategy.

DR. KENT BERRIDGE, like almost all neuroscientists in the 1980s, assumed the dopamine system was, essentially, a pleasure system. This made intuitive sense. I want this T-shirt, this car, this glass of scotch, *because* I like it. So, Wanting and Liking were two points on a single timeline. Making twin gods of Wanting and Liking would have been especially easy to do in the eighties, of course—it was the zenith of free-market euphoria, a time when greed was good and desire was conflated with well-being.

Berridge hypothesized that, since dopamine produced enjoyment, he could reduce a creature's ability to enjoy things by lowering their dopamine levels. And he set out to prove just that. Thirty albino rats were assigned to the experiment. Rats are ideal for studying enjoyment because, like human babies, they display their reactions to food in obvious ways; rats will lick their lips when they enjoy their food and shake their heads or wipe at their mouths when they do not.

Berridge and his team anesthetized his rats and drilled small holes in their skulls. Using a hypodermic needle he could then target the bundle of dopamine fibres in each rat's hypothalamus and inject it with a neurotoxin called 6-hydroxydopamine, which knocked out their dopamine neurons. In effect, Berridge was aiming to create rats incapable of wanting or enjoying anything a rat ought to want or enjoy. Apathetic, mirthless rodents.

Once the rats had convalesced, they were each lifted from their living quarters and placed in a transparent Plexiglas chamber (a sort of large aquarium) for observation. They were given mounds of food and plenty of fresh water, but the dopamine-free rats wouldn't take a bite or sip. *Ah, thought Berridge, their pleasure has been drained. My rats can't enjoy food they would have pounced on before.* The old theory seemed to hold; dopamine controlled enjoyment.

The rats began to starve. Berridge surrounded them with food but still they would not eat. Finally, to keep his subjects alive, Berridge resorted to using a gastric feeding tube, intubating condensed milk down each rat's throat—the same technique used for feeding premature human babies that cannot suckle. And then Berridge noticed something extraordinary. As he nursed each rat they began to lick their lips. The rats were, in fact, clearly enjoying their food, desperately enjoying it. Yet they would take no steps on their own toward consuming more. The rats would stare past any treats as though they held no promise. They *liked* the food enormously—but they could not *want* it at all.

Was it possible that Wanting and Liking were entirely separate brain functions? The idea flew in the face of received wisdom and Berridge didn't quite believe what his results were suggesting.

In 1990 he launched a second experiment with the hope of putting the matter to rest. A new team of albino rats was enlisted. This time, instead of dismantling their dopamine systems, Berridge aimed to ramp them up. Pin-sized electrodes were implanted in each rat's hypothalamus so that stimulating jolts could be administered to their dopamine neurons.

Berridge and his team delivered fifteen-second zaps and, each time, the rats would pounce on their food, guzzle their water, and manically mother their young. Berridge watched for symptoms of increased enjoyment; there were none. In fact, just the opposite occurred. While the rats were compelled to consume more resources, compelled to want, they were wiping their mouths and shaking their heads—signs of displeasure. Disgust reactions even bled into their experience of rare sweet treats. The rats enjoyed everything less, even as they wanted everything more.

"In the 1990s, this was a lonely scientific position," Berridge told me as we discussed his experiments. The proposition that Wanting and Liking were not tied at the hip was a serious disruption. By way of context: the eminent Dr. Robert Heath, a couple decades earlier, had made a homosexual man "want" sex with a woman by boring electrodes into his "pleasure centre" and zapping him during intercourse with a female sex worker; this was proposed as a cure for the patient's homosexuality because Heath imagined Liking something was the same as Wanting it. But Berridge's rats had upended that tidy supposition.

It would be a further decade, though, before the scientific community believed Berridge's rats had something to teach humans. The tide seemed to change when Parkinson's patients were given dopamine-enhancing drugs (to offset the degeneration of dopaminergic neurons) and began compulsively gambling, eating, and shopping without deriving any new sense of fulfillment. Dopamine, the "molecule of more," was driving them to consume without any reference to their well-being. Indeed, when humans were later fitted with neuron-stimulating electrodes, just like Berridge's rats had been, they compulsively hit buttons to give themselves jolts—hit those buttons thousands of times in a row when allowed—but never once did they "like" it.[60]

To want is not to enjoy. And the difference between these two states is not merely a matter of time—wanting first and enjoying later; it is a difference in basic functionality and utility, a difference in value and meaning. Yet we constantly conflate the two, thinking the pursuit of what we want is interchangeable with the pursuit of happiness and well-being. (This is akin to the economist who thinks that GDP can measure a country's whole health.) So, those of us with the privilege of consuming whatever we choose are often tripped up by our own biology and led by want alone. Saddled with such prodigious, bottomless desires, we hoard shoes and gadgets and lipsticks; we book flights to Puerto Vallarta, upgrade our data plans, and plant rare grasses by the curb; we stare at Aston Martins and dig into the crumby bottoms of Doritos bags with the same insatiable need to gather, grasp, gain. All the while we edge toward—what? Not, in the end, the secret fulfillment of a heart's desire, never some lasting point of bliss, but instead another lap on the merry-go-round—frozen horses, a looping song, and an endless pattern of lurches. Because to want is not to enjoy. Berridge told me we can obsess over unnecessary consumption "with the same compulsive urges that a starving person would have for food." And yet no satisfaction is required, nor conclusion.

The Wanting part of the brain, it turns out, is much larger and more robust than the Liking part. Our desires are capacious enough to eye the petroleum of Qatar, the rice of China, the palm oil of Indonesia, and on and on. Utilitarians will tell you these hungers are based on just two factors—safeguarding a pleasure or avoiding a pain. But we are not so rational and not nearly so simple. Our wants can run counter to well-being. In fact, our lives are riddled with contradiction and self-destruction. We may even destroy a planet for a few more years of material comforts.

What are we, then? Just a crowd of animals with haywire compulsions? Just more of Berridge's rats, torqued this way and that by invisible forces? I see I've twice used the word *just*, as though a full, mature human would be beyond all this. We like to think so. But who really lives beyond the body's gears and mechanisms? A worm searching three feet underground has her private, driving wants. We, too, are only creatures.

AND THEN I am back at my city's landfill, thinking about the story again, how it shapes us, grooms us. I think about the story while watching the roaming trucks shape and groom all that garbage into pretty, rounded hillsides that will be covered with soil and finally scattered with Lynn's flower seeds.

A question occurs to me and it feels like a small opening:

If we're trapped in a story that's about to end, is it really our chemistry that keeps us from jumping toward a new one?

I'm tired of only thinking in terms of dopamine, tired of blaming our obsession with the consumer story on unchanging "human nature" (whatever that is). Our stories about life are always human inventions in the end, mutable—replaceable. We cannot merely wave a despairing hand at our wiring and stop there, because if the world is collapsing thanks to "human nature," then we've already given in to a mythical Fate—and there's no need to.

4

THE BERNAYS FACTOR

HE BELIEVED IN America, in the story of America. He believed in growth like a green sprout and in tomorrow; in his own future and in the future of his country; that he would be a self-made man and that a man like him—one so optimistic and so injected with energy—could also shape the lives of others. He did not look the part. He was short and sinewy, with grey-blue eyes and a caterpillar moustache, a funny-looking man who could not easily get three people to listen to him. But no matter. Edward Bernays did not care about the attention of this man or that woman; he cared about people as a mass, how they flocked. That was where his attention lay and that was the bent of his genius.

Edward Bernays was raised in a New York brownstone and came into his own just as America emerged—aspiring and industrious—from the First World War. For a time, he was a press agent for the famous opera singer Enrico Caruso and, having proven himself adept at stirring up a crowd, was enlisted in the nation's propaganda effort when President Woodrow Wilson went to Paris for the 1919 peace conference. There, the twenty-eight-year-old Bernays worked to portray Wilson as a liberator of the people and was fascinated by the ease with which this could be accomplished. The masses tidily complied with the propagandist's version of events. Was this magic limited to war propaganda, though? The enterprising Bernays thought surely not; there must be room, too, for propaganda in times of peace.

"Propaganda got to be a bad word," he would later explain. "So what I did was to try and find some other word."[61] On his return to New York after the peace conference, Bernays coined a term, *public relations*, and declared himself *not* a propagandist after all, but a public relations counsel. The move was savvy; America's companies were going to be desperate for new ways to relate to a newly enriched generation of consumers.

THE AMERICAN TOBACCO Company, for example, which made Lucky Strike cigarettes, had a woman problem. It was easy enough to get men to smoke cigarettes (the trenches of World War One had made them into emblems of male prowess); men smoked on the street, in theatres, in restaurants, and at work. But women only smoked at home and in private; they weren't smoking nearly their share. And so in 1929 American Tobacco's president, George Washington Hill, called "public relations counsel" Edward Bernays into his office and barked at him, "We're losing half our market because men have invoked a taboo against women smoking in public. Damn it, if they spend half the time outdoors and we can't get 'em to *smoke* outdoors. . . . Can you do anything about that?"

"Well, let me think," said Bernays. Then, having thought, he said to Hill, "Have I your permission to see a psychoanalyst?"[62]

The shrink at the top of his list was Sigmund Freud himself, who had the added distinction of being Bernays's uncle. Bernays had grown fascinated by Freud's theories about the unconscious forces driving human behaviour and he believed his public relations work could harness those forces for business interests. In letters from Vienna, though, Freud showed little interest in his nephew's mercantile pursuits. Bernays was able to secure a Freud disciple instead—an American called Dr. A. A. Brill who, for a very large fee, was willing to inform American Tobacco that cigarettes were really abstracted penises. Because the penis is equated to male power, he went on, whenever oppressed women acquire one they find themselves holding "torches of freedom." To smoke, concluded Dr. Brill, is to be liberated.

"Torches of freedom" struck a nicely patriotic note, recalling the Statue of Liberty with her own torch held aloft. Bernays liked the image and decided it was his job to unite the female smoker with the ideals of freedom and liberty. He only needed to somehow fuse the abstract with the concrete, the idea with the act. He needed to write a chapter of the consumer story that flattered and involved the American woman.

Long before Instagram influencers, Bernays knew the value of a good word from "the right sort of people." And so, from a friend who worked at *Vogue*, he acquired the names of thirty New York City debutantes. Telegrams were sent to each, signed not by Bernays but by his secretary, Bertha Hunt, who neglected to mention any corporate sponsor. Her telegram began: "In the interests of equality of the sexes and to fight another sex taboo I and other young women will light another torch of freedom by smoking cigarettes while strolling on Fifth Avenue Easter Sunday."[63] Each debutante was invited to join Ms. Hunt and display their allegiance to the women's liberation movement. Together, tomorrow's women would slough off the strictures of yesteryear and embrace their independence.

Only ten debutantes showed up but that was more than enough for Bernays. At the appointed hour the women strolled down Fifth Avenue in their black leather Mary Jane shoes, puffing as they went. Bernays, meanwhile, had alerted newspapers that a team of suffragettes was engaged in a photo-worthy protest. Photographers were duly dispatched and captured the scene: ten respectable women in pearls, felt hats, and wool coats; ten good-looking but (as per Bernays's instruction) not "model-y" women; ten enviable but relatable women smoking in public with relish, taking a stand together for women's rights. Bernays made sure the reporters had the tagline, too— those weren't cigarettes the women were smoking, those were torches of freedom. When reporters inquired as to the origins of the event, Bertha Hunt told them it was all "spontaneous"; the fingerprints of Bernays and American Tobacco were nowhere. In fact, Hunt elaborated, she wasn't associated with any firm but had come up with the idea for the march out of pure indignation—it was high time somebody stood up for the freedom to smoke where one liked.

The sensational images ran in papers across the country, sparking a nationwide "debate" that was hardly contentious at all—for who would come out against liberty? What American would dare take arms against freedom itself? Bernays had set the terms and, in doing so, had cracked a powerful new formula: consumer goods could be promoted not just for their utility, as had been done in the past, but as symbols in a larger narrative, ways for the consumer to situate themselves in life's drama. Cigarettes became icons of the flapper generation's power and independence.

Within weeks, American women were smoking in more and more public places—the female hand could artfully dangle a cigarette in a pose of confidence and control. And Lucky Strike, which was poised with a female-centric ad campaign, took the lion's share of the profits.

JUST A FEW months earlier, President Herbert Hoover met with a group of men from the burgeoning ad industry. He told them: "You have taken over the job of creating desire and have transformed people into constantly moving happiness machines. Machines which have become the key to economic progress."[64] Up until that point the majority of people, if they were advertised to at all, were shown goods that had concrete uses, basic necessities. But Bernays and his peers were discovering the Freudian shopper, a consumer blessed with a little extra cash and an endless desire for a starring role in modern life. Other schools of psychology were exploited, too: members of the behavioural school (which thrived in America) were hired by ad companies that hoped to elicit Pavlovian responses in shoppers.[65] The newly rich consumer public was a gold mine from which profits could be extracted if one only knew the method. A senior partner at Lehman Brothers, Paul Mazur, echoed Hoover's call for "happiness machines" when he wrote that year, "The community that can be trained to desire change, to want new things even before the old have been entirely consumed, yields a market to be measured more by desires than by needs. And man's desires can be developed so that they will greatly overshadow his needs."[66] America was shifting from a needs-based to a desires-based culture. Shaping a new mentality, transforming people into happiness machines—the influence implied is wizardly. But so optimistic, so brazen, were the roaring 1920s that one did feel able to wring desires from the air, concoct new levels of consumption using nothing but human ingenuity. It was an audacity that belonged to a marvellous twentieth-century world.

Hoover's word choice—"happiness machine"—is telling; it reflects an increasing reliance on machinery in general.[67] Wealthy nations in the West had, since the seventeenth century, been investing more and more in mechanized mass production, until a whole factory culture had emerged. Consider that, in the nineteenth century, new multi-spindle spinning frames ("spinning jennies") allowed one worker to spin cotton on eight spindles at once, causing the price of cotton products in Britain to collapse by 90 percent between the 1790s and 1830.[68] As ever, efficiency in production invited a ratcheting up of consumption: the sales of textile products soared. Many similar production booms arrived at the start of World War One, with advances in machinery massively cheapening the production of other goods. But in times of peace those machines could only be kept running by increasing consumer demand. Citizens had to become invested in a "purposeless material-ism,"[69] an aimless growth—or growth for growth's own sake. All those fantastic new machines constantly increased the production of goods, drove down their costs, and so (in order to capitalize on each new production level) it became neces-sary to constantly increase the public's desire *for* those goods, too. Ad men became the chief scribes of the consumer story and they elaborated that story so ornately that, as Mazur prophe-sied, *need* was replaced by *want*. A calculus of desire was born.

AFTER EDWARD BERNAYS'S "torches of freedom" stunt, women were smoking more Lucky Strike cigarettes than ever. But not enough to satisfy George Washington Hill. So, in 1934, the head of American Tobacco called Bernays back into his office and said their market research had sussed out another problem—women felt *allowed* to smoke in public now, yes, but they didn't like the Lucky Strike packaging. They felt the forest-green boxes were garish. A simple enough problem; Bernays suggested they change the colour to something more neutral. But Hill refused. He'd sunk millions into that green; it was the Lucky Strike brand. Bernays barely blinked: "If you won't change the colour of the package, change the colour of the fashion."[70] Women's taste would be made to align with the brand, rather than the reverse.

Once again, the "right sort of women" were enlisted to execute Bernays's plan. This time he went to Narcissa Cox

Vanderlip, a wealthy suffragette who was chair of the New York Infirmary for Women and Children. Wouldn't Mrs. Vanderlip's infirmary like a donation of milk for starving infants? Wouldn't clothing for the poor be appreciated? An anonymous donor, Bernays told her, was waiting in the wings. They wished to raise funds at a marvellous charity ball—a Green Ball, say— produced by the anonymous donor and hosted by Mrs. Vanderlip herself. Bernays managed to hide from her the fact that Lucky Strike was behind the scheme. And, eager to raise funds for the infirmary, Vanderlip agreed, quickly involving her well-heeled friends, too (her acquaintances included the wives of Irving Berlin and FDR's son, James Roosevelt).

In the months leading up to the Green Ball, Bernays executed a flurry of manoeuvres to ensure that New York City became obsessed with the colour green. In Larry Tye's book *The Father of Spin*, he recounts how retailers were warned that a green wave was imminent and they ought to stock more green gowns, shoes, and jewellery; magazines and newspapers, egged on by Bernays, declared green the "it" colour of the year; a Green Fashions Fall Luncheon was organized where fashion editors dined on green beans, asparagus, pistachio desserts, and crème de menthe; and, most ludicrous of all, a Color Fashion Bureau was hastily set up in order to assuage worries about green clashing with interior decoration (the Bureau at first courted attention by issuing announcements to department stores and interior decorators, but soon it was being independently approached for its chromatic advice).

Green filled the pages of *Vogue* and the windows of Fifth Avenue shops. When the day of the Green Ball finally arrived, each woman in attendance was obliged to wear a green gown, which sparkled under specially installed green lights in the Waldorf-Astoria's ballroom. By all accounts Hill and American Tobacco were extremely pleased; the fashion had been changed and Bernays received a bonus. As he dryly remarked: "emphasis by repetition gains acceptance for an idea."[71] Taste itself was a thing to be directed; the consumer's reality could be engineered by the insistence of a few men in search of profits.

HOOVER'S VISION OF American citizens as "happiness machines" whose gears could be operated by Bernays and his fellow ad men would set the tone for a century's worth of consumption that was barely ever bridled; a century where "happy people" and "industrious factories" enjoyed a long, symbiotic affair. And this affair would only grow more intimate as liberal capitalism proceeded to triumph over fascism, over communism, over every alternative narrative. By the end of World War Two, America's capitalism was the loudest story on the planet and its plot described the "new necessaries" of life: cars, washing machines, refrigerators, toasters, vacuum cleaners, an entire fleet of devices to please, to ease, to empower, but most of all to *define* the consumer who became, with each purchase of a "new necessary," made over into a well-functioning happiness machine. Meanwhile, cleanliness standards increased, ensuring that housewives worked as much as before—or more.[72]

The machine this consumer became was also a moral machine, one not associated with decadence but rather with clean living and a healthy soul: a "prosperity gospel" arose in the 1950s to teach American churchgoers that if you committed yourself to the Lord, he'd make you wealthy in return (this echoed Max Weber's idea that capitalism was tied to the Protestant glorification of industry). Material wealth became a sign of spiritual strength. Kenneth Hagin, founder of the popular Word of Faith movement, was a leading light of the prosperity gospel and preached that the same God whose son was born in a manger now wanted his followers to "wear the best clothing. He wants them to drive the best cars, and He wants them to have the best of everything."[73] And so, there was no need for consumer culture to supplant that other grand narrative, religion; it could absorb religion instead.

As our moral selves were folded into the consumer story, so were our political selves. American sociologist Daniel Bell looked over the burgeoning consumer society and announced that it had done away with old narratives that were "infused with passion" like Marxism and nationalism. Those earlier narratives had been pseudo-religions, offering guidance and patching over rifts in disparate societies. Such passionate dogmas were necessary throughout the nineteenth and early-twentieth centuries but, in an America of glorious abundance, they were no longer needed. And good riddance: "A total ideology," wrote Bell, "is an all-inclusive system of comprehensive reality, it is a set of beliefs, infused with passion, and seeks to transform the whole of a way of life."[74] Bell felt it was time to move beyond the wretched passions that had dragged millions into two world wars. America in the 1950s, rational and clear-eyed, could drop zealots, icons, and idols, and clutch a shopping bag instead.[75] Bell may have underestimated, though, how consumerism could become a total ideology of its own. Ad men like Bernays, after all, were learning to subtly flood the population with a kind of background radiation, a story that shaped, coloured, penetrated the culture. They were learning to marinate every corner of modern life in their consumer narrative—until its simple directives (buy, use, toss) became an ideology of the everyday.

Having shopped for all the accoutrements of modern life, the twentieth-century American was not just supplied with things, but a complete self. They ascended into a plot as spiritual and satisfying as any of the old ideologies; they had subscribed to a narrative that imbued life with meaning and purpose. They became one with the story of their time.

DO OUR PURCHASES really become part of who we are? A Tesla Roadster, a Gucci jacket, a bottle of thirty-year-old Macallan: perhaps none of these improves us ... but doesn't each possession exert a miniature tug of psychic gravity? Don't they move you, change you slightly? The philosopher William James, who died just before Bernays came on the scene, believed that we each have several components to our selfhood and that a "material self" is among them. His material self included the body but also our clothes and the contents of our homes—everything external to the pure, thinking self that lives inside our heads.

William James came from a wealthy, intellectual family (his brother was the novelist Henry James), but his privilege did not save him from his body's regular betrayals. James was an invalid as a young man and grew suicidal; later in life he was plagued by heart problems that eventually killed him. Perhaps it was all this physical hardship that brought his attention to such earthly matters; chronic sufferers have daily proof that life is more than an ethereal experience.

James was incredibly well connected (he knew Mark Twain, Ralph Waldo Emerson, Bertrand Russell, and Carl Jung) and very well established, too (before turning to philosophy he taught anatomy at Harvard), so he was in a rare position to upset social norms while being taken seriously. He did believe in the traditional idea of a soul, a nucleus called "I" at the heart of each person's experience. But to this "I" James added a "me," which included all those material components. Our clothes, our possessions, our *things* are constituents of that "me."

"This me," he wrote, "is an empirical aggregate of things objectively known."[76] The soulful "I" at the heart of us, the "I" that does the thinking and extends through past, present, and future to stitch together a coherent self, is constantly appropriating all those material things the "me" is made of. James insisted that we are more than god-given souls trapped inside bodies like fireflies in a jar. Rather, we are various and multiple, composed of things internal and external; the self is aggregate and impure.

He noted that, "We feel and act about certain things that are ours very much as we feel and act about ourselves."[77] And this intimacy with our things hints at the way we bleed into them. They "may be as dear to us as our bodies are, and arouse the same feelings and the same acts of reprisal if attacked."

A shattered bedroom window, a lost wedding ring, even a scuffed sneaker can make us feel vulnerable because our self-hood partly resides in what we claim as our own. Ad men like Bernays encourage this intimacy between ourselves and our things. They encourage us to pour some part of ourselves into each possession; if those possessions are lost, we are prompted to feel "a sense of the shrinkage of our personality, a partial conversion of ourselves to nothingness."[78] Perhaps each of these miniature losses is an intimation of that greater loss—our death, when we lose our most valuable material treasure, the body. Perhaps it hurts so much to lose a coffee mug, a book, a toy, because it reminds us that nothing material is everlasting and we will one day forfeit even our flesh and bone.

If losing things can feel like we're losing ourselves, the opposite also proves true. Buying new things gives us a sense of being renewed. Purchases often feel like a completion, an affirming of the self. We paint self-portraits and each purchase is a stroke of the brush. We buy things in order to make solid our vaporous qualities.

Bernays attached women's liberation to Lucky Strike cigarettes. Today, an ad from Procter & Gamble features Black parents explaining racial bias to their children;[79] an ad from Audi shows a father worried about the gender pay gap his daughter will face;[80] an ad from Apple exhorts the viewer to take care of our precious ecosystem;[81] and a Pepsi commercial shows Kendall Jenner achieving world peace by giving a handsome police officer a can of soda.[82] Choosing this brand or that signals an allegiance. So, as consumption choices multiply, the shopper is supposedly shaping not just their own identity but society at large. In reality, of course, the society that has been bought into being is not one that celebrates women's liberation or racial equity, or environmental care. The only society that can be bought into being is a society of consumers.

BY THE LATE 1990s, this blending of the self and what we consume was complete. Not only did we learn to imbue products with personality and soulfulness, but we reimagined our souls as products themselves. Business guru Tom Peters argued in the magazine *Fast Company*, "Starting today, you are a brand. You're every bit as much a brand as Nike, Coke, Pepsi, or The Body Shop . . . being CEO of Me Inc. requires you to act selfishly—to grow yourself, to promote yourself, to get the market to reward yourself."[83] And so we were not merely *attended* by our consumer goods anymore—we were rebuilt in their image.

The CEO of Me Inc. can only be successful by becoming, in Peters's words, "the brand called You." To compete for jobs one must shape a persona with the same focus and ruthless maintenance of a consumer brand. The old company man, tethered to monotonous and long-term employment, became a nostalgic figure; no longer would a single factory or office carry you through to a sweet retirement. A generation was destined, instead, to leap between a dozen jobs, with none of them providing for long-term well-being. Therefore, as Peters explained, our *real* job must be to promote, sell, and push a personal brand. That is the one constant, the thing you can hold on to in a precarious market. And this, to be clear, was an exciting thing. No more corporate ladders! No more old-fashioned hierarchies! Raised to believe we were special, we each secretly believed our personal brand would outshine the rest. And each new adoption of corporate-speak brought our identities closer to the consumer products we loved. A new age arrived where the self was a flattened thing to be sold, where people became avatars and where political stances, aesthetic choices, even tone of voice, would be marshalled into a product indistinguishable from merchandise. It is no coincidence that children raised to think of the Brand Called You wished to become movie stars, pop singers, and YouTubers, while their parents had opted for "teacher" and "doctor."[84, 85]

The brands now dominating our lives (Apple, Twitter, Facebook, Google) are not merely products we "align" with but the platforms that give rise to our being, the oxygen supporting every Brand Called You. And the intimacy of social media's ad ecosystem would have thrilled Edward Bernays. On TikTok and Instagram, individuals long to become influencers and wield some small slice of the branding power that traditional ad companies enjoy. For a minuscule minority this leads to celebrity and sponsorship. The rest become "nano-influencers," destined to be collected by studios and sold in bulk to brands looking for pre-packaged cheerleaders. A certain low-calorie beer or Hawaiian hotel can thus enjoy a flood of "authentic" testimonials on demand. Brands as mainstream as Uniqlo and Sephora rely on these swarms of selves to shape online opinion in exactly the same way Bernays relied on New York City debutantes.[86] Peters's supposedly independent Brand Called You is thus cannibalized by corporate interests and made into a

Brand Called Us. Each "me" still feels special, of course, for the platform does allow your face, your avatar, to shine. Indeed, the image of an authentic self is the very thing being mined. But influencers, all these fresh-faced entrepreneurs, know they must still hone themselves into tiny notes in a global media racket.

Meanwhile, this same fantasy—that there is no space between the "real you" and the brand you are aligned with—is brought to life in makeover reality shows like *Queer Eye*, where mavens of consumption coach slovenly participants toward shinier, happier lives. (To be clear: I enjoy *Queer Eye,* and it would be truly marvellous to live in a world where a home reno, a $200 haircut, and a pass to Orangetheory were all it took to unlock personal transformation; but I watch such programs precisely because, like all efforts at spiritualized consumption, they are glittering fantasies.) After the camera crew has packed up, each participant must have a quiet reckoning, a moment where they wonder whether they've merely performed "change" for the TV audience. This is the branded self's constant anxiety: we become obedient actors for our so-called followers; the more we win the game of "Me Inc." the more we lose track of that quieter, unbranded "I."

I doubt that many of us set out to be defined by such glum role-playing. And yet that nervous status is exactly what contemporary life so often encourages, not just on reality shows but on the crowded boulevard, on the glossy magazine page, in the teeming Instagram feed; we are always cajoled to become more *aware* of all the other striving souls and to prioritize their gaze.

This anxiety about status and belonging can only be alleviated by more consumption. So, consumer debt balloons as we strive to meet the mark. In the US alone, consumer debt edged toward $15 trillion in 2020.[87] Two thirds of that debt belongs to mortgages, and a great deal of the remainder belongs to credit card debt (a category that expanded after a 2005 act made it harder to declare bankruptcy in the States). And all this new debt *also* sutures us to the story of consumption, of course, for we are never so invested in a story as when it has taken something from us. Most of capitalism's lovers know they have really arrived at "the good life" when they are saddled with a million-dollar mortgage—which, while not so parasitic as credit card debt, still forces the owner to believe in a property's unimpeachable value (if your home is *not* worth your life savings then that would make you a sucker). Historian Yuval Noah Harari describes this "mysterious alchemy of sacrifice" by which a debtor becomes *even more* invested in consumer goods because they have surrendered so much at the altar: "Most people don't like to admit that they are fools. Consequently, the more they sacrifice for a particular belief, the stronger their faith becomes."[88] We love the consumer story all the more as it grows monstrous and absurd.

Advertisers live at the threshold of that monstrosity, targeting the individual with more and more precision, until we forget where our selves end and the atmosphere of consumption begins. Targeted advertising in the digital age is so personal it weaves into the motions, thoughts, and patterns of ordinary life. In 2017, for example, Google began shipping "beacons" to businesses that use their advertising services, part of an enormous campaign to make ad-targeting more precise. It works like this: the beacons (small white blocks that could fit in your palm) are placed in hidden locations around a store; they emit Bluetooth signals to any nearby phone; if you've downloaded the store's app in order to score a few bargains, that app can be triggered by the beacon; the beacon now knows who you are (you agreed to that when you downloaded the app) and it sends your location to a server; there, your location in the store is cross-referenced with your past buying habits and other personal data that Walmart, or whoever, has managed to scrape together (maybe your income, your exercise habits, etc.); an appropriate advertisement can then be issued to your phone, suggesting you purchase that yogurt you love, which is still within arm's reach and—*ping!*—is now 50 percent off.[89] With extraordinary ease, the shopper is nano-targeted to within a few metres and presented with intimately curated delights. Google has told app developers their beacons "give your users better location and proximity experiences," but "better" is a proxy here, for "shop-inducing." The rhetoric is charming: with beacons you can "help users' devices to discover content and functionality"—as though no corporate "functionality" were at play.

Whether via Google beacons or Instagram stories or Facebook feeds, the free platforms that dominate our online lives make sure to always point toward purchases. Advertising, as author Tim Wu points out, "is the ultimate point of aggregating so much attention in the first place."[90] And every exciting new service is eventually revealed to be one more way to target consumers with greater finesse—when Facebook's "like" button was introduced in 2009, for example, the platform was not issuing a fun feature for our enjoyment, it was installing a powerful data-mining tool that monitors our preferences so they can be monetized. As social platforms evolved, users were enlisted to produce content for and about themselves—which has the advantage of making users produce market research. Inflammatory posts are encouraged, flame wars and outrage mingle with lustful adoration, and all that crowdsourced content is marshalled to explain the beliefs and wants of the population at large—it all exists to serve the advertisers who fund the platform. Our very lives are grist for their mills.

There's an old joke that people in sales used to tell: "Half my ad money is wasted, I just don't know which half." Targeted, personalized ads solve that problem by singing directly to us. Many of my friends are so struck by the exactness of ads that they're convinced their phones are spying on them—how else to explain the discounted flight ad that pops up minutes after Cancun is mentioned in conversation? The spying theory may be paranoid—but it's at least an honest paranoia. When we're constantly and intimately targeted, when we're cajoled into believing that we've been made into a Brand Called You, how could we not suspect that all our acquiescing, all those tiny branded moments, have finally added up to a wholesale takeover? But the truth may be even more unsettling: those ads aren't matching our desires; our desires are matching those ads.

A SEARING (if indirect) response to the Brand Called You arrived in Naomi Klein's book *No Logo.* Klein was in her twenties when she wrote her manifesto, and she spoke for a generation that was at once a target for branding machines and primed to rebel against their influence.

Her book launched in December 1999, just days after the start of the World Trade Organization Ministerial Conference in Seattle, where tens of thousands of protesters alternated between riots and demonstrations in a "Battle of Seattle" that brought globalization and corporate greed to the forefront of the national psyche. Klein and her international readership had watched McDonald's and Microsoft and Nike elbow their way into everyone's headspace, demanding more and more attention and influence as they grew. Smaller businesses were throttled, workers' rights were ignored, sweatshops in faraway countries operated unjustly and in obscurity. Klein saw that brands could proceed with a measure of impunity because our growing identification with them often made us complicit with corporate ugliness.

It even became possible to shift the onus of ecological responsibility away from lobbyists and their polluting companies onto the consumer. "We" were destroying the planet, not a group of marketers and paid-off politicians. As Klein would later argue, we came to accept "maddening invocations of 'human nature' and the use of the royal 'we' to describe a screamingly homogenous group of US power players."[91] Brand identification—the absorption of the self into a consumer narrative—was so valuable to corporate brands precisely because it moved corporate responsibility onto the shoulders of consumers.

It was a trick they'd been playing for decades. In the 1950s, after disposable containers were introduced and became a source of garbage, the Keep America Beautiful organization was created by leaders in the packaging industry, along with Coca-Cola and Dixie Cup, to shape the narrative around the garbage their products created. Keep America Beautiful admonished Americans to stop being "litterbugs," neatly shifting the blame away from those who made single-use products and onto those who bought them.[92] The same thing happened in the 1970s when governments in rich countries regulated recycling efforts: to salvage used-up material became a kind of personal atonement, another way to shift responsibility away from corporations and onto individual citizens. "Recycling," says historian Frank Trentmann, "has been little more than a comforting distraction from the stuff that really matters."[93] Litterbug campaigns and recycling campaigns are not the radical change we could demand from policy-makers and corporations.

The lie of brand identification—the insidious way it passes the buck—relies, though, on a certain gullibility from individuals. And what Klein and others have argued is that we aren't half as gullible as the Edward Bernayses of the world had hoped.

BEFORE SMOKERS HAD irrefutable proof that cigarettes caused cancer, strokes, and heart disease, they did know firsthand that smoking could irritate their throats. American Tobacco paid opera singers to refute that experience, though, and endorse Lucky Strike with claims that cigarettes, in fact, "soothed" their throats. Edward Bernays, meanwhile, produced press releases touting the ultraviolet "toasting" of their tobacco, which "gives you a cigarette free from harsh irritants." This strategy was dramatized in the show *Mad Men* when Don Draper concocted "It's Toasted" for Lucky Strike. "Advertising is based on one thing," Draper explains: "happiness." And what is happiness? "It's the billboard on the side of the road that screams with reassurance that whatever you're doing is okay." Even if part of you knows it'll kill you in the end.

Bernays attacked early research on harmful effects, arranging for scientists to pen pro-cigarette counterarguments, even while he forwarded to his employer abstracts from medical journals that exposed the health risks. "I do feel," he wrote to them, "that serious attention should be given to the problem of having ready a strong offensive." And yet, decades later, in 1972, an aging Bernays excused his work for American Tobacco by writing in the *Boston Globe* that cigarettes back then were considered "kind to your throat. Opera stars endorsed them." Had he forgotten those endorsements were a sham? Drunk his own punch? His biographer reminds us that "he had good reason to suspect the perils of smoking as early as 1930."[94] Far from being ignorant of the truth, Bernays purposefully designed a truth of his own. He encouraged American Tobacco to bury newspaper editors in conflicting reports filled with what we now call "alternative facts." The goal was to create so muddy a landscape that editors who received an anti-cigarette story would "hesitate to print it because they [had] been convinced of the contrary point of view."[95] Without a stable set of facts, he hoped, the consumer would be unable to make choices of their own. And he did have a certain terrible kind of success. It was decades before consumer patterns caught up to the facts on the ground. I'm left wondering whether, somewhere along the line, he also fooled himself, forgot that his story was only a story.

Perhaps the only reality Bernays cared about was the aggregate purchasing patterns of the masses. But he would discover, in the end, that each individual can be a stubborn, wayward thing—that we each may defy an ad man's wishes. His wife, Doris, was a pack-a-day smoker and, in the privacy of their home, Bernays was desperate to make her stop. He never smoked himself and knew it would be her death. He hid her cigarettes, told their children to hide them, too; he snapped them in half; he flushed them down the toilet. All to no avail. Doris continued to disobey her husband by doing what he'd worked to make all other women do. But her addiction had one further complexity: adding insult to self-injury, she chose her own favourite brand—Parliament.

STORYTELLERS—for all their skills—can be defied.

5

ALL WE NEED

KING PHILIP OF Macedon wanted his palace dripping in gold. All the mines of the Balkans were his, after all; one day all the world would be, too. Why shouldn't his people squint in the light of so much glory? Why shouldn't every object within his reach be the finest, the most precious and rare? Why, indeed, shouldn't all things reflect back to King Philip the sheer awesomeness of his person? Was he not a kind of noble element himself—very like the gold he coveted? Statues of Philip were erected at a scale formerly reserved for the gods.[96] He was an almost-divine being, a ruler in the grandiose style of the Persian monarchs he so enviously eyed.

Philip's people spoke the Greek language but they were "new Greeks"—only Hellenized a couple generations earlier and considered rough by the Athenians to the south. There was no political culture in Macedonia, no independent judiciary or parliament—only Philip with his untold wealth and absolute power, only this king compelled to prove his worth. It became necessary to collect the best of all the world and make each treasure his own—the greatest poets and scribes were called to his side, cultural baubles for his court. And, naturally, when King Philip's son Alexander needed an education, it was decided the child should be tutored by the greatest living philosopher. A message was sent to Aristotle.

Aristotle had, himself, been raised in Stagira, a small city-state in the north of Greece, not too far from gilded Pella, where Philip had his throne. His parents both died when he was a teenager and, shortly afterward, he became Plato's star pupil in Athens—he lived there twenty years, gaining steadily in skill and renown. By the time Prince Alexander was ready for tutoring, Aristotle had precisely the status that King Philip admired. The philosopher was forty-two years old and (despite his fame) without much wealth, so the appointment would have been financially tempting. But dangerous, too: King Philip's court was decadent yet lethal, glamorous yet wicked; his concubines and lieutenants were constantly murdering and extorting each other as they jockeyed for position. Still, one could not safely say no to such a ruler. So, in 343 BCE, Aristotle went where he was bidden.

Young Alexander would one day become a brilliant military strategist and fulfill his father's dream of running rampant over Persia, but there is no real evidence he was much of a philosophy student. Tutoring the prince (along with other noble Macedonian youths) would have been unsatisfying for Aristotle, and the gig dragged on for the better part of a decade in a grossly despotic court—the philosopher became one more ornament collected by King Philip II. Experts tell me it's amazing Aristotle survived so long in such a violent milieu, full of literal backstabbing (a true Game of Thrones). But perhaps we should not be surprised. He maintained an aura of indifference; he wasn't enmeshed in their wrangling for power and he was apparently impervious to bribes and affairs. (Also, while he *was* a northern Greek, Aristotle was not technically Macedonian, which may have lessened any threat he posed to the purebloods.) The major hardship he suffered at Pella seems to have been the company he was forced to keep. And even that had its upside: he was able to observe the elites in action, could see first-hand how their wealth and power made them miserable. Those years in the royal court taught Aristotle how the cream of society curdles; they were not, in fact, living "the good life."

The conclusion of Aristotle's employment would underline that point. In the autumn of 336 BCE, King Philip walked into a theatre in the city of Aegae, wearing fine white robes, and was stabbed to death by Pausanias, one of his seven royal bodyguards. The guard may have been involved in an elaborate coup devised by Philip's wife, Olympias, and Alexander; it's also possible the guard was aggrieved when the king (a lover of his) refused to avenge his honour after Pausanias was raped by others in their circle; we do not definitively know his motivation. Aristotle himself barely mentions the event in his writings; his employer's murder does not seem to have interested him much. We do know, however, that all the gold from all the Balkan mines did not protect the king.

Philip was slain, and the assassin was slaughtered in retaliation; Alexander ascended to the throne and took his army to Persia in search of blood. In Hollywood's version the philosopher goes east with Alexander; in reality he did not. While the Macedonian court rolled to glory and the prince became Alexander the Great, Aristotle went quietly south to Athens.

There, only a year after Philip's death, Aristotle founded a school called the Lyceum, stationed at a temple devoted to Apollo. Free from courtly intrigue, he was able to formalize and record his work. Aristotle looked back on his years in Philip's court and found all the murdering and intrigue a suboptimal approach. How was it that the wealthiest, most privileged people seemed so often miserable? He proposed that they spent their lives pursuing precisely the wrong sort of things. Most people, in fact, sought power, fame, and material comfort—imagining these outward signs of success could lend real purpose to their days. Aristotle chose a very particular word to describe his *alternative* goal, the thing we ought to be pursuing instead: eudaimonia. When I first heard that word—*eudaimonia*—I was struck by its beauty on the lips. It took me a week to learn how difficult a word it really is.

OFTEN, EUDAIMONIA IS translated as "happiness." But is Aristotle suggesting that being happy is the point of it all? That we shouldn't pursue honour, kindness, commitment, or any other virtue? Looking over the self-help options at bookshops, you might imagine happiness really is the only measure of a life. And certainly happiness is what's on offer in every advertisement, too: *buy this thing and happiness shall follow*. A state of blissful contentedness is the reward all promotions, all bargains and sales, promise.

Other translations give us a bit more definition. Eudaimonia is "flourishing," it is "blessedness," it is "felicity." But none of those words quite satisfies, either. We still seem to be circling a state of "being pleased," a state of satisfaction that a person could arrive at with a tidy certainty.

In his *Nicomachean Ethics*, Aristotle gives a further hint by telling us to seek an activity of the soul.[97] And, with that, the secret of eudaimonia begins to crack open. An activity of the soul is not some prize we can win, it's not a thing we can get. "Activity" implies an always becoming, a mode of being, a practice, a habit.

"I see it as very much a verb, not a noun." Edith Hall, the celebrated classics scholar and author of *Aristotle's Way*, spoke with me from her home in London; she agreed that translations of *eudaimonia* are always "impossibly ropy, really." But her grammatical insight untangled things for me. "It's not a state," she said. "It's something you *do*. You *do* eudaimonia." This is, of course, far removed from the consumer approach, where well-being is something we *get*. And the opposite of everything King Philip stood for. "It's *verb*-al," repeated Hall, growing more excited now. "It's a way of life and a set of behaviours that you decide, quite consciously at first, to implement. You do it in daily interaction with your family, your co-workers, your fellow citizens, the rest of the world. And these ways of behaviour actually do become habitual." But *what* "ways of behaviour," exactly? Aristotle had his own theory as to which activity is paramount: we must lead a life that lets us develop our reason, he says; he believed reason is the defining human attribute and therefore our *humanness* shines when we develop that quality.

We each are tethered to our own circumstances, though, our own environment and faculties, and so we each have our own work to do. Psychologists Edward Deci and Richard Ryan write that eudaimonia is expressed differently in each of us, because "well-being is not so much an outcome or end state as it is a process of fulfilling or realizing one's daimon or true nature—that is, of fulfilling one's virtuous potentials . . ."[98] My virtuous potential may vary from yours—and perhaps it varies within the course of my life as well. And yet there *is* something solid to hold on to here: the idea that the meaning in our lives derives, in fact, from a lifelong, habitual "activity of the soul."

This work, whatever its exact course, "takes a complete lifetime," Aristotle tells us, "for one swallow does not make a summer."[99] So, our well-being, our eudaimonia, is not something humans can ever achieve. It cannot be grasped. Rather, a good life must be spun into being every day and every hour.

We mistake this matter at our peril. The assumption that life is a game one can win leads to disaster. Ovid gives us an example of that disaster in the story of Midas, the king of the Phrygian people, who returns a lost satyr to the god Dionysus; so overjoyed is Dionysus that he offers Midas anything he wants as a reward. Like the clever child who says he would wish for "infinite wishes," Midas wants the ability to turn everything he touches into solid gold. Dionysus consents, and Midas, pleased with himself, anticipates a life of extreme wealth, power, and fame. He touches the branch of an oak tree and it turns to gold; he touches a rock and it goes golden, too. So far, so good. When he gets home, though, Midas orders his servants to prepare a celebratory feast, which, of course, he cannot eat; his food turns to gold as he lifts it to his lips. A goblet of wine turns to golden ice. Midas frowns at his riches while his stomach grumbles; he begins to curse the gift that was so recently his delight.

When Nathaniel Hawthorne tells this story (in the nineteenth century), the curse of material greed is made even more explicit: Midas's daughter comes to the king and complains because he's been walking in the garden, turning her roses to gold, and now the flowers have lost their beautiful scent; Midas instinctively reaches out to console his daughter and she, too, is destroyed. As with King Philip of Macedon, Midas has a love of material conquest that leaves him divorced from humanity, isolated from life itself. Undone, he begs Dionysus to take back his terrible gift. In some versions of the story, the god relents and reverses the spell.

When Aristotle tells the story, Midas dies of starvation.

WE ARE ALL potential Midases now. As Hall told me: "People mistake the happiness that can be temporarily derived from spending a thousand pounds at Harvey Nichols for actual gratification." She was not, though, arguing for a wholesale reversal of consumer culture. Even Aristotle recognized that all societies need a certain level of production and trade in order to function. "Everybody has to be a grown-up," Hall said, "and decide what that level is for themselves." But, Aristotle warns, the moment you have a surplus of goods, you're in trouble. "He seems to be saying that we do not want economic growth," Hall said. (And so here was a classical analogue to Jørgen Randers and his *Limits to Growth* report.) Aristotle, in fact, studied the history of over a hundred city-states and found that extreme economic growth, and the income disparity that always attends such growth, is toxic; he proposed a ratio whereby the wealthiest person in a given society may have five times as much as the poorest; any greater disparity leads to civil misery. "It's not saying that we've got to have a total economic levelling, you know," Hall clarified. "It's not levelling. It's just a sensible ratio beyond which emotions will get out of control."

When Hall mentioned that ratio, though—where the wealthiest have five times the wealth of the poorest—I laughed out loud.

"Yeah," she said, "I know . . ."

"I mean, where does that leave us? The average CEO in the States makes *three hundred* times more than their workers."[100] The absurdity of our situation, when held up against Aristotle's proposition, struck me anew. In the past couple decades, the wealth gap in the United States has more than doubled.[101] Income and wealth inequality is further exacerbated every year (and disasters like the COVID-19 pandemic only magnify the effect). It is estimated that, if the federal minimum wage in the States had kept pace with the country's economic growth, it should now sit at $24 (but, in fact, Americans have struggled to even raise it to $15).[102] Stating the obvious, I said, "We're massively out of whack."

"We have lost the plot."

"What do you think Aristotle would have to say about our lives in the twenty-first century?"

Now it was Hall's turn to laugh. "Horror. Certainly horror that you end up being ruled by economic algorithms. You hand over control . . . I think he would have deeply admired the sort of social democracies that people had in Scandinavia in the post-war period."

"I know he's not giving us a self-help book—"

"No."

"But do you feel he can help us redefine our goals, at least?"

"Not *re*define. Define in the first place. People don't think: *What do I get to do with my years? What do I do with my years and how do I behave?*" But a little Aristotle, she hopes, can nudge us toward those questions. "I go around to schools and kids will lap up philosophy and ethics. Fifteen or sixteen is the ideal age to get them on this and try to stop them going down the consumer route." Hall sees philosophy as crucial to our survival as the old game of the twentieth century tumbles apart. "It's all so shit for millennials. I'm horrified by what young people face."

In the summer of 2019 she travelled to Crete as the guest of former Greek prime minister George Papandreou and met with some exceptions to the millennial struggle: twenty-five hand-picked "future leaders of China" had come to Greece in order to learn about Aristotle. This was part of their preparation for political careers and Hall felt an enormous responsibility—to a man, they were young oligarchs coming of age in a China not especially favourable to Aristotle's view. (China's institutions are more friendly toward Plato and his idea of a trained political club.) "They genuinely believe," Hall said, "that democracy will never work because people uneducated in political science shouldn't be given a vote. They genuinely believe it ... but I think perhaps two of them I made some impact on. I was trying to teach them a sense of personal, secular ethics." Her task was not unlike Aristotle's when he tutored young Alexander. Like Aristotle, Hall was shipped in, a global expert for hire, and provided for the illumination of tomorrow's kings. To bring philosophy to a group of young men who had known nothing but the richest and finest things in life, to get some of the most privileged youths on the planet to ask fundamental questions about life's purpose *beyond* their enormous wealth—the task was daunting.

"Well," I said, "if China goes especially sideways, I'll know who to blame."

She groaned and we sat in a brief silence while my joke twisted in the air. Why was it so ridiculous, I suddenly wondered, to think a little philosophy could improve these future leaders, maybe even help them shape a saner world? Was it really so hard to believe people can discover a new story about life's purpose, that they could adopt a new narrative? Was I calling her work useless? I did still want to believe—*had* to believe, for the planet's sake, for humanity's—that our stories can change mid-life. I needed to believe that reason, argument, a few convincing philosophers, could help a person swerve from the precarious road to Midas-town. I was sorry, then, for making light of Hall's efforts. Penitent, I put my questions away and we spent the rest of our time together talking about spouses, children, the illnesses of loved ones.

I HAVE READ that the Aztecs were utterly convinced the sun would stop moving through the sky if they ceased making human sacrifices. Their story felt that important. Today, though, nobody's still-beating heart is offered up to the gods and the heavens manage to keep from crumbling. Stories end and the world, oblivious, turns. Things that call themselves natural turn out to be merely customs. And customs can be changed—policies change them, laws do, wars, natural disasters, technologies, viruses ... We are now stepping into the proof that our consumer culture is only one idea of how a life can be measured. Change is always possible once we shake the idea that history is over.

The idea is a stubborn one, though. In 1989 a thirty-six-year-old deputy director of the US State Department's policy planning staff, Francis Fukuyama, published an essay titled "The End of History?" It was an elegant, sweeping argument, the sort that these days would be delivered via TED Talk. "History," in Fukuyama's view, was essentially one long ideological evolution toward the endpoint of Western-style liberalism. In the same way Daniel Bell had cheered our evolution beyond "passionate ideologies," Fukuyama saw the inevitable collapse of the Soviet Union and the Berlin Wall as the final ideological hurdles, beyond which lay the promise of capitalist democracies for all. The West had discovered the final, perfect story. And it was now clear that history had simply been a march toward the realization of human freedom, an inexorable journey whose terminus was Fukuyama's consumer-driven America. He wrote that history had "culminated in an absolute moment—a moment in which a final, rational form of society and state became victorious."[103] It's common enough for a young man to think of history as one long preparation for his own existence, but this took the idea to new heights. The late twentieth century was, Fukuyama suggested, the beginning of our true destiny, the beginning of an everlasting and finished reality. The essay was an immediate phenomenon, selling out the magazine's print run and becoming the talk of the town among D.C.'s intelligentsia.

There were, though, immediate detractors. Christopher Hitchens rolled his eyes: "At last, self-congratulation raised to the status of philosophy!"[104] Fukuyama's argument that there were no new ideologies on the horizon seemed to only pan out if one ignored the prospect of a newly industrialized China or the revival of religious fundamentalism or, for that matter, the plight of the developing world where his version of "history" had only just begun. Fukuyama's essay, it seemed, pointed less to the conclusion of a grand historical arc and more to the myopia of the culture in which he was steeped. And, despite his announcement, History did not end. The idea that it *had* ended was, itself, only an onion-skin page rapidly turned. The historian Gertrude Himmelfarb perhaps did the best job of undoing the confusion: No, she demurred, the American Dream was not the goal to which Planet Earth had forever been conspiring. Every reality is merely a reaction to whatever came before it, and is itself something to react against down the line. "The synthesis of the preceding stage is the thesis of the present," she wrote, "thus setting in motion an endless dialectical cycle."[105] In other words, we live forever inside yesterday's consequence. New dramas, new narratives, are as inevitable as they are surprising.

And so we're left to synthesize the old consumer story and wonder what our own thesis could be. Are we stuck as President Hoover's "happiness machines," humming and well-fuelled, obedient and beholden? Or will we vote, protest, riot, *choose* an alternate story? If we're careening now into a future where, like it or not, consumption patterns cannot hold, how long before we stop blaming "human nature," or ad men, and start imagining our new lives into being? We may discover our generation's mission if we finally admit that what came before was not the conclusion of history but only the inspiration, the instigation, for what comes next.

I THOUGHT A long while about the idea of eudaimonia, the idea that an activity of the soul was the only sure path toward fulfillment. I thought maybe Edith Hall was right and an ancient philosophy did have something to tell us about how to survive the twenty-first century. It seemed to me that consumer culture was constantly offering to fulfill us with things captured and killed. More gold for King Midas, more baubles for King Philip. But never lived experiences. Never practices, nor habits. That was what I was after next: stories that could satisfy human needs without relying on the dead glory of oil, the allure of cigarettes, the doped-up rush of Instagram and Twitter. Stories about building a self, hour by hour. I wanted stories that could survive this precarious moment. I wanted stories that disowned the perfect life I'd been promised and instead embraced the daily, ordinary miracle of life itself.

PART II

Stories

6

STARS FROM
UNDER THE WAVES

THEY SAY THAT, midway through life, blurs appear. Garbled meaning where purpose used to be. Frightened, some of us buy Porsches and jewellery to distract ourselves from the senselessness. But most struggle along in smaller, less dramatic ways. We turn forty and rearrange the furniture. We ask ourselves what we've been chasing, and why. We begin to imagine course corrections.

When I turned forty I was midway through this book. My research into the creation of the consumer story had left me impatient for a way out—another story to embrace. But when I encountered what seemed to be alternatives, I saw them through a blur.

The first blur smudged my vision because of a craftsman. I was walking my dog one afternoon through a lane filled with workshops and I stopped to watch a woodworker building a simple dinghy. Here was a quiet mastery, a devoted quality—and a sense of purpose totally foreign to me. I knew nothing about what it meant to build with your own hands, to watch wood or clay evolve under human guidance. But something was fascinating about this person's steady work, his calm presence. Then came the blur, the sense that an obvious part of life was missing.

In that neglected space where my understanding should have been I found an illegible message, an impression of cultural memory that I couldn't read in full. There are these hollows in our understanding. We know there are other ways of being, other stories, and yet we can't quite . . .

SO, I BEGAN staring longer at those blurred spaces. Partly out of my desire for a richer view of things but also out of prudence—it seemed obvious that new modes of being would be required to survive the twenty-first century. We live by our stories and, if we can't bring new narratives into focus—stories beyond the grand fairy tale of consumer culture—then we are doomed to live out of sync with reality.

At first they refused to resolve at all. There was a blur where I should have understood Craft: the way the natural world is shaped by human hands. Another blur appeared where I should have experienced the Sublime: a relationship with the transcendent. And then another—the most painful—appeared where I should have understood Care for other people. Each time, the air shook with a need to know and I was set to work again, sketching things in my notebook, trying to find the signal through the noise. I barely understood at first what drew me toward those broken signals. Nor did I understand what they had in common.

All I knew was that the stories that started to emerge out of those blurry spaces promised something vital, a new way to tell my life what it was. If I did my job, they might even offer structure and purpose. The rest of this book is devoted to those stories—they make up my survival pack for life beyond consumer culture.

I am still only learning to read these stories. I read them through a haze, the way a fish looks at stars.

7

CRAFT

I'D BEEN STEWING in my research for maybe a year. This meant reading, and interviewing experts, and annoying my husband with repeated talking points at dinner. After being so obsessed with the problem of consumption—its *stickiness*—I'd only just begun to look for an opening, a way out.

Then, one day, I was travelling down a YouTube rabbit hole—Donald Trump was shouting at a rally, Neil Patrick Harris was giving *Vogue* a tour of his townhouse—and the algorithm's strange magic offered up a video that did not fit. An elderly man was crafting a birchbark canoe in a wooden shack. One hundred and forty-five views. Maybe because it reminded me of the man I'd seen weeks earlier, building his dinghy, I clicked.

The video seemed out of time, out of place. And I had the feeling again that I was viewing a kind of blur—a noise where there should be signal. The man's voice was crackling, lolling, slow, as he explained his expert motions. I leaned in. He seemed wizened, peering up with ice-blue eyes to explain each arcane fact about his work.

Something about the man in the video came as a relief, or perhaps it was permission I felt, permission to be interested in something outmoded and quiet, something remarkable and yet unmarketable. There was a bland reverence for his mate-rial, a calm attention paid to the natural world. I was confused by my own interest. But it felt, anyway, like the beginning of an alternative—the first line of a story far removed from the con-sumer story, one this strange man was telling himself. I decided to go find him.

HIS NAME TURNED out to be Don Gardner and he kept a workshop somewhere in the Canadian Rockies near Banff, though I wasn't sure exactly where. I'd been told it wasn't much larger than a single-car garage. In it, he built birchbark canoes using ancient methods and, over the years, he'd grown region-ally famous for the beauty of his work. I wanted to visit and learn what makes a person do something so needlessly diffi-cult, what makes a person settle into labour when a machine (or a quick shop on Amazon) would do the trick.

I had proposed a visit and Gardner had agreed. After flying to Alberta, though, I asked for an exact address and he wrote back, "Address? Oh, right, you're city folk. North side of Policeman's Creek. You can smell the compost if there's west wind by the raven's nest." This was an inauspicious beginning.

Was Gardner, I worried, merely a caricature of the old-time craftsman? Was he play-acting out here in the woods and about to regale me with screeds against modernity?

I found Policeman's Creek, glacier-green and winding, and hiked beside it a couple hours. Far off at its source there were mountaintops, painted with blue haze and great swatches of cloud-shadow. The pines all around were distinct and lean in the midday sun. Things seemed to be growing more precise. Each sight and sound was highlighted, drew out an ecstatic, foolish appreciation—for the water, the woods, the blood-red depth of chokecherries. At last I came upon a ramshackle building painted white with a spearmint trim. One window was boarded up with plywood. Don Gardner's workshop.

It used to be a warming house for a skating rink twenty kilometres away, but one winter the locals skidded the structure down the frozen river to its present location. A scud of smoke issued now from the little chimney.

"Hello?" I knocked and heard a chair scrape.

"You're here! Yes, hello! Sorry!"

Inside, an elderly man was stationed by a wood-burning stove, licks of grey sticking out from his ball cap. The room was warm and smelled of fresh-cut wood. There was also an herbal note trailing from the Tolkienesque pipe in Gardner's hand. He crinkled an apologetic smile and puffed. "Just finishing my morning spliff."

Gardner had me sit in a chair draped with the long-haired skin of some animal. Under my feet there were skate-blade dents from the building's former life. He sat, facing me, in a plastic lawn chair by the fire. Over his shoulder, in a jumble of timber and bark, lay the unfinished skeleton of his next canoe, which I was eager to get talking about. But Gardner seemed less interested in the canoe and instead, after our introductions, he handed me an odd, pointed object. "Siberian harpoon," he said. "This would be added to a two-metre-long shaft with some do-dos, some gizmos."

The harpoon head was made of two kinds of bone fitted together, one marbled with caramel, like a sweet latte, the other more raw, like old teeth. "This is narwhal tusk," he said, touching the caramel. "And this is walrus ivory," he touched the other. "It comes apart inside the animal. When you hunt a whale, say, this would pull off and there would be a rawhide line. You would be out on the water in a kayak or umiak, big skin boats, and this would be in the animal, and your line would lead back to a float made of sealskin. The skin is so finely sewn that you can blow it up like a balloon." His eyes bulged at the thought. "The whale would then be dragging around this balloon for two or three days, which the hunter could chase. It would take that long for the whale to be exhausted, at which point they could paddle up and lance an artery or something."

I mentioned, here, the conversation I'd had months earlier with Professor Lieberman, how he'd described our ancestors' endurance hunting on the savannah, how higher dopamine levels allowed them to outlast their fleeing prey. Gardner nodded, it was all one to him. "The same principles are there, all over the world."

I liked Gardner immensely, liked his circular, searching speech, the humility with which he picked up a piece of wood or bone. Gardner was raised on the Canadian prairies, climbing poplar trees and lampposts. He was a child of nature, and, in the spring, would float on miniature ice floes down Calgary's Elbow River. From youth onward, he seemed to intuit that beneath the material obviousness of the world lies a treasure of memory and myth. He wanted to meet that treasure, face it. At nineteen, he skied for twenty-one days over three hundred kilometres of ice fields and mountain peaks, from Jasper to Lake Louise. An unprecedented trek. Later, in his forties, he skied for twenty-nine days from Canmore to the Pacific Ocean, sleeping each night in the dry wells at the base of snowed-in trees.

In his shack I leaned back, felt the scratch of fur at my neck, and took in the crowded space. What seemed at first benign—five-foot-tall scrolls of birchbark, fistfuls of curlicued shavings on benches and windowsills—grew more macabre the closer I looked. My eyes jumped between piles of sawn-off antlers, the still-bloody leg of a deer, a hide stretched torture-style on a rack, a creature's foot dangling from a pegboard. There were also photographs, books, curiosities everywhere. On one bench, two enormous planks had been painted over with Mayan scripts and gods. I must have been staring.

"That's from Guatemala and Mexico," he said, walking over to show me. I scribbled in my notebook. "You'll be dizzy after you leave here," he smiled.

"I've got a feeling I'm in the presence of a Renaissance man."

"Is that what they . . . somebody said that and I don't know what . . . were they bad or good, those Renaissance? I want to be good."

"I think they were curious, is what they were."

"Well, good, yeah. I am really curious, yeah." Gardner scrubbed his face and tugged down his ball cap. "Ever since I was a kid, I wanted to play with sticks and rocks, and make fires, the joy of it all." The other children used to call him Grub Gardner because he was always in the dirt. "I was making gliders, and boats, and dams. I guess I was a maker. That feeling's been important to humans for a million years, I guess. But we wash it away pretty quick when we grow up, we wash away that basic intrigue, of looking at a stream and going, *I belong here because I can build a raft for that.* A feeling of being immersed." He turned to me. "I guess I'm still a child. I stayed that way."

GARDNER'S WORLDVIEW FEELS like something the rest of us left behind in the nineteenth century.

In 1851, England's Prince Albert joined forces with the inventor Henry Cole to produce the Great Exhibition—an inaugural World's Fair that assembled the splendours of the manufacturing age within Sir Joseph Paxton's Crystal Palace in Hyde Park. Among its thirteen thousand exhibits: a Jacquard loom, to automate weaving; a reaping machine, to automate farming; kitchen appliances, to automate food preparation; daguerreotypes, to automate picture-making; and so on. The future ushered in by Prince Albert would be fresh and brimming with fast copies of whatever you wanted. It was an undoing of craftwork like Don Gardner's. The joy of the future, in fact, would be our ability to become clueless about the made-ness of things; instead we'd revel in their speedy production, their mint condition. The Great Exhibition was a testament to a new consumer paradise, an economy we could all buy into. Karl Marx visited and found: "With this exhibition, the bourgeoisie of the world has erected in the modern Rome its Pantheon, where, with self-satisfied pride, it exhibits the gods which it has made for itself."[106] The slower production of traditional craftwork was pilloried by Prince Albert's modern fair and the new, industrialized economy it heralded. By contrast, the Arts and Crafts movement that briefly flourished in reaction to industrialism—the florid textiles of William Morris and the stained-glass windows of Charles Rennie Mackintosh—was championed by socialist thinkers who wanted to support the workers of the day, workers being elbowed aside by machinery.

The value of making, our esteem for it, recedes in an age of automation. Our machines cycle through material at a blistering pace—letting us consume flatter, faster, cheaper versions of furniture, clothing, and gadgets, until we end up in an imaginary moment that pretends to have no past at all. Instead of the sculpted vessels and handmade clothes that were, for millennia, at the centre of human lives, our things become mysterious, wrapped in plastic, and unsullied by human touch.

Automation of one sort or another permeates my life—from my breakfast cereal, which was prepared and packaged by machines, to the mattress I lie down on at night, which was manufactured by robotic arms and delivered via an algorithm's directions. Meanwhile, staff at call centres are replaced by chatbots; production lines go mechanical; job applicants are winnowed by software; checkout cashiers are replaced by self-serve stations; operating systems repair their own files; the list goes on. We naturally embrace all this ease. And yet we also have little choice in the matter. By the mid-2030s, a full third of today's jobs are expected to be automated away (a shift only amplified by the job-shaking effects of the COVID-19 pandemic).[107, 108]

Employers are often excited by this prospect; to many of them, employees are a costly evil best avoided. And that avoidance is easier than ever. Compare two photography companies, for example: the Kodak film company employed 145,300 people at its peak in 1988;[109] but in 2012, when Instagram was bought by Facebook for more than a billion dollars, it employed only thirteen people.[110] Immense value can now be created with a fraction of the human labour that was necessary before.

Those whose jobs remain may find their work segmented and stripped down. In Adam Smith's famous pin factory example, the multi-step process of making pins is divided among specialists so that the end result is arrived at with as much speed and efficiency as possible. Comprehension of pin-making is dissipated in the process and each worker becomes a mere component of a larger, automated endeavour. The "system," in other words, knows how to make a pin, but the worker does not. What would Smith think of today's global online marketplace? It allows for so much division of labour that humans can be atomized into obscurity. The enormous breadth of Amazon's marketplace compels that company to produce fleets of warehouse employees who move packages about, as ordered by machines instead of managers; Uber's mammoth marketplace produces drivers who simply go where their phones tell them. The scope of work is narrowed and arenas of human labour that were once more engaging inch toward annihilation.

Economists do not complain about this shift any more than employers do; they are satisfied to watch automation wring more and more GDP from fewer and fewer people. When economists talk about the "productivity" of a country's workers, they are calculating the GDP per hour worked. One can even imagine an entirely unemployed population in possession of profit-generating supercomputers; such a population would be "highly productive" even if everyone stayed in bed. Some economists would cheer. Our GDP may happily climb all the while but we would be left with the surprisingly difficult task of coming up with something to do.[111]

IN PLACE OF LABOUR, some offer us a "universal basic income," a stipend of cash or free services fuelled by machine-made wealth. And we may be closer to such a dramatic reorganization than many suspect. Global labour force participation has been declining since the 1990s.[112] Redistributing our collective wealth to the unemployed in a world of increasing automation is evolving in the public's mind from a supposedly socialist fantasy to a pragmatic proposal. But is it also a vision of diminishment? What expenses go untallied in this deal? Will we bother to measure the disappearance of agency and skill and participation?

What actually happens to those of us who are removed from our labour? In addition to the obvious risk of lethargy and depression, we may grow divorced from a whole strata of experience, including knowledge of how things are made and why they are ordered as they are. Work, in its finest expression, is always a manifest curiosity, a looking into things, and an engagement; to have no work at all—no job, nor hobby, nor labour of any kind—is to consign oneself to an incurious state of passivity. (Anger, too. Our dopamine makes the pursuit of resources integral to us; strip us of something to strive toward and we will soon rebel.)

Aristotle (along with the Buddha and others) felt human labour was much more than a necessary evil; to him it was a way for each of us to exercise our faculties, stretch our muscles, grow into our own potential. If we agree with Aristotle that the good life is achieved through an "activity of the soul" then the work we set ourselves may be part of that activity, a daily coming into being. Economist-philosopher E. F. Schumacher compares this ancient truth to modern fantasies of leisure-centric lives when he writes:

> To strive for leisure as an alternative to work would be . . .
> a complete misunderstanding of one of the basic truths of
> human existence, namely that work and leisure are com-
> plementary parts of the same living process and cannot
> be separated without destroying the joy of work and the
> bliss of leisure.[113]

But what is "the joy of work" that Schumacher holds up here? Most of us spend our shifts with one eye on the clock, wondering how soon we can return to family, friends, and the comfort of Netflix. "Joy" seems to be the thing we get *after* work. Even the supposedly inspired among us—the poets and painters—spend more time chasing invoices and pursuing part-time gigs than they do rapt with the pleasures of creation.

The psychologist Mihaly Csikszentmihalyi has proposed that, if we can only spend more time with work that captivates us, our well-being will be unlocked. But a hundred barriers may prevent this unlocking, including poverty, disabilities, and illness. Many of us feel consumed by dull, unfulfilling labour. Our jobs are often a torturous economic necessity, not some exercise in personal fulfillment. Yet economic labour is only one kind of labour. Good work often exists outside the economic system and includes our passions for baking, gardening, and any number of hobbies. If we can love the process of *some* task more, if we can nudge ourselves toward investment and curiosity in the work we love (be it paid or unpaid) we may slip into what Csikszentmihalyi calls "flow," a state of ego-less satisfaction. The anxieties of everyday life fall away, time ceases to drag, and we become both lost and found in our task. He describes a blessed, semi-aware state that leaves us not drained by labour but revitalized:

> Contrary to what we usually believe, moments like these, the best moments in our lives, are not the passive, receptive, relaxing times ... The best moments usually occur when a person's body or mind is stretched to its limits in a voluntary effort to accomplish something difficult and worthwhile.[114]

We should not wait for our employers to build such fulfillment into our days. They have been taking their time at it, if they're interested at all.

The malaise of our times is partly the result of thinking that the instant consumer rewards that our jobs make possible will somehow balance out years and years of disengaged, unfulfilling labour. We often focus—hopefully, gullibly—on those end-stage prizes, making grudging allowances all the while for the drudgery and boredom we're consigned to in the meantime. Everybody, however, deserves the chance to pursue Aristotle's activity of the soul. And if our employers do not provide such activity, we can pursue it on our own.

GARDNER AND I left the nook by his fire and examined the unfinished canoe that dominated the shop. Its rib cage had been built and beneath it lay the unattached skin—an enormous roll of birchbark whose pores ran down one side like bird tracks in snow.

"How do you choose the bark?" I asked.

Gardner thought a moment, pulled his cap bashfully over his eyes. "Well, I guess it's almost the way you go into a bar. I'll circle. I'll get the vibe. If I'm in the bush and I see a beautiful tree and the sun is shining—well, the south side of the birch will be smooth and pale and in the sunshine it's beautiful like a girl in a bar."

"How thick is this bark? Not very."

"About three millimetres. Any thinner and it won't be strong enough for a boat; any thicker and you can't shape it. Thickness is crucial."

Everything turned out to be crucial. Any question I had about a material or process led to not just answers but stories, philosophies, a whole correct attitude. There were fine lenticels and ungainly ones, scars from fallen branches that changed possibilities, perhaps twenty pertinent attributes in all, any one of which could disqualify a tree. Gardner has a spot, hours from his workshop, where the boreal forest on the side of a valley has just the right drainage and the trees are just the right age. (He wouldn't tell me exactly where.) It can take him a full day of trekking through the wild before he finds the right tree, puts up his ladder, and cuts away the outer layer with his four-inch knife, prying the bark off while leaving the tree's vital sap system intact.

"Of course," he suddenly said, "all this is kids' stuff, it's nothing to a bow." And he thumbed at the bench behind me. I turned. Nesting among baroque curls of shaved wood were two carved bows, one made of yew, the other of elk antler. I looked at the sticks, and back at the grand canoe I'd come so far to learn about, and back to the sticks again.

"Should we talk about the bows instead?" I asked. Gardner moved at once and fished around in a pile of old bones, extracting the severed bottom half of a deer's leg. The hoof, black and solid, had an inch-long trim of toffee-coloured fur; the rest was skinned and sheared of meat, just two jointed and bloody bones fit for broth. In this bit of gore Gardner prodded with the tip of his knife until a kind of thread emerged just below the animal's "knee." It came off the bone with a satisfying pull like a fleshy bit of cheese string, and I shuddered, thinking of the sinew at the back of my own leg.

Gardner stepped up to the bench and I saw now that amidst the mess of shavings, there were other dried strips of sinew like the one he'd just harvested. Bow makers, I would later learn, have been combining wood and sinew for centuries. Native Americans in California hunted with sinew-reinforced bows, as did nomads of the Asiatic steppe.[115] Sinew has a tensile strength four times greater than the wood used to make a bow; fixing the two materials together is a kind of alchemy where the animal's strength and the wood's form unite. Composite bows are another option, with horn added to the mix, increasing the compressive load the bow can bear. Centuries of tinkering, and deep intimacy with materials, allowed our ancestors to arrive at these solutions independently in various parts of the world. When scientists at Bell Labs worked to figure out mathematically perfect bow designs in the 1930s, they arrived at solutions that matched bows created by Neolithic people.[116]

Gardner picked up a single string of sinew from his bench and popped it into his mouth to moisten it. Once he was satisfied, he took the yew bow and pressed the sinew into a network of hundreds of similar strands. Wood, sinew, and saliva combined.

"Have you been working on this one a long time?" I picked up the other bow to see if I could balance it on the edge of my finger.

Gardner took it from me and laid it down again. He pinned his eyes on it and swiped at the wild sides of his hair. "I've been working on that one for fifteen years."

DON GARDNER UNDERSTANDS the reality of an elk antler in ways I cannot fathom because, like every craftsperson, he must reckon with the reality of his material. A leather worker does not *hope* to tan a strip of leather by applying what *feels* right; she reaches for the chromium sulfate. A potter does not *wish* that porcelain could be fired in a microwave; he sets the kiln to 1,300 degrees Celsius. This respect for the reality of nature helps us avoid destructive fantasies that place human want above ecological truths.

When we constantly disregard the material authenticity of things, when we live for digital facsimiles and obliging reproductions, we train ourselves to stop respecting the real costs, benefits, timelines, and laws that govern the natural world. And to do away with such cares is to become thoughtless about environmental impact. Craft is a cure for such a heedless mindset. It trains our eyes to marvel, and not just when we study wood and stone.

All life steps into a new light when we learn to look around with interest. Focus your gaze to one small dot of attention with an electron microscope and the eye of a fruit fly becomes a field of balloons and spears; an eggshell becomes an expanse of burlap; a snail's tongue is the florid appendage of an alien. A whole magical apparatus turns beyond our understanding: beyond humanity's sensory array there are sounds we cannot hear, sights we cannot see, and scents we cannot smell. Pressurized magma produces infrasonic harmonic tremors that our ears don't catch; X-rays and gamma rays and microwaves all do their business in light invisible to our eyes; African elephants have five times our olfactory sense receptors and can smell miles-away water. The world "as it is" has more signals and miraculous characters than we will ever comprehend. And it matters whether we maintain a state of reverence for those miracles because they add up to a support system providing oxygen, carbon sinks, medicines, and nutrients. If we cannot find an interest in all that, we risk abusing and destroying it.

It's easy to be tempted away, of course. Life is now one long reception of finished, opaque products whose material underpinning is hidden from us. When I set myself to work on this book, for example, I ordered a little forty-dollar table from IKEA, which I screwed together and set up in my "office," the staircase landing. Its components were perhaps manufactured in China, or Vietnam, or Myanmar. It is impossible to say. There are more than a thousand vendors that IKEA works with, spread across fifty countries, and learning what went into what is a fool's errand. I know my table's legs are steel, that its top is a honeycomb of cardboard encased in a shell of melamine. But when I contacted IKEA to learn who made it, where, and with what, I met a wall. Months of back-and-forth messages, months of promises from their communications department and subsequent silences, got me no further. It was, apparently, a bizarre and difficult request.

It shouldn't be. Our respect for what goes into our things should not be limited to the handiwork of artisanal furniture makers; indeed, understanding the history of my mass-produced desk matters more. IKEA, after all, uses more of the world's lumber supply than almost any other retailer (they even bought their own eighty-three-thousand-acre Romanian forest to keep up with demand).[117]

Only by applying the craftsperson's care and attention to mass-produced goods can we hope to account for the fragility and beauty of the base materials with which we build our lives, the inherent value of the planet's resources. There are material realities, after all, invisible yet prodigious, beneath every cheap T-shirt, every hamburger, every WhatsApp message; beneath the glittering facades that industrialists and ad men prop up, beneath all the received pleasures of consumer culture, there is still rock, water, dirt—thirteen septillion pounds of necessary planet.

If we took that material world seriously, we would, I think, be less eager to destroy it.

GARDNER WRUNG HIS hands and lowered himself down by the fireplace. "In my dotage—that means my old age ..."

"Got it."

"My dotage—well ... Hm." He took another run at the idea. "I used to find the magical in the landscapes I would hike through. And now I'm finding it almost everywhere. It's right here. I can smell it. I can hear it. I can touch it through the ... sensorium." He looked proud at finding the word, smiled right at me. "Sensorium." He nodded and repeated that the magic was everywhere now, in the simplest things on Earth and also the most complex. His next workshop, he told me, will be out-of-doors so that he can work the way his ancestors would have, in the changing air.

His work had made him feel at one with a large, profound planet. He had a role *in* that world, a vocation, one that could not be taken from him. I suspect that when jobs become vocations, when we love our labour with such intimacy and such an attachment to the materials on hand, then the work can provide us with a sustaining narrative, a story about who we are.

The German word *Bildung* is useful here; it means both "education" and "formation" (in English literature we have the *Bildungsroman*, a novel that describes a hero's formative years). The craftworker's *Bildung*, their daily accretion of skill and observation, literally informs their personhood, prepares the practitioner for the life they are to lead. In other words, a lifetime of loving labour, a devotion to slow and involved learning, has meant that when Don Gardner wakes he knows where he is going—to his workshop—and that mission makes, to him, an implicit sense. His is a reassurance I never seem to have, a honing that I wish had shaped me, too. As much as his craft seemed like a sensible antidote to a consumer culture's waste, I saw now it was also a kind of psychic relief, an enviable mindset that he could enjoy and I could not.

A knock at the workshop's door drew our attention.

"Sorry," Don said, "I always answer." He opened the door, welcoming a man he introduced as Chris.

"Are you a canoe?" Chris asked me, nodding at the half-made boat. For a moment I thought he was insane but then I realized he meant a person who works on canoes.

"No," I said. "A writer."

"World-famous!" added Don. "And Chris here is world-famous for being partly blind and . . ."

"Crippled," offered Chris.

"Crippled!" Don repeated. (I wasn't sure whether this was a joke.)

We spoke a while, the three of us, about random acquaintances of theirs, and then Chris, who used to work in wildlife preservation, stepped over to one of Don's benches and picked up a horn.

"That was roadkill, I think," said Don. "A bighorn sheep." He winked at me.

"It's very fast," replied Chris. And, again, I was at a loss. People were canoes; horns were fast. His language was secret, strange, shorthanded beyond the grasp of amateurs like me.

Don tried to remember the animal that grew the horn. "Maybe it was eight or nine years."

"Oh," said Chris, "that's very, very fast." And now I understood he meant the horn was fast-growing. "I don't think you'd get that around here," he continued. Chris held the sheep horn up for my inspection and I saw he was describing the rings of growth that demarcate the animal's life, with darker rings signalling times of stress. The horn was a hardened record of trauma, prosperity, and famine, and Chris was able to gauge the animal's health, what kind of food it had eaten; he could even guess which mountainside it had roamed. Their conversation went on like this, full of obscure observations that were actually signs of a finer understanding of reality than I'd ever reached for. As faraway and antique as their sensibility seemed, it also struck me as a smart survival strategy for the twenty-first century—since our time demands a greater awareness of the wood, wind, and sun that support us.

So here was a story, coming into focus. The blur I'd felt before seemed to, for a moment, resolve into something distinct and real. Something to hold on to. It was a story about hands reaching out, exploring, trying, learning. A story about walking out and meeting the world. The blur was gone and, watching the two of them pass the horn back and forth, I felt I was watching something old as humankind—and brand new to me.

LATER, AS I DROVE back to the town of Banff, where I was staying, the Rocky Mountains loomed more ominously than before. The highway wove through a valley with mountains on every side, mountains robed by a slanting, bronzed light, sinister and darkening. And it struck me, in that light, that I'd seen those mountains before. The range dead ahead was treeless, a billion-year-old shelf of exposed continental crust, an enormous layering of limestone and shale. It was the Earth tearing skyward to expose its own subcutaneous tissue. And then I knew where I'd seen it—or imagined it: all that marine snow gathering in layers at the bottom of ancient oceans. I thought, too, of the striated sheep horn in Don Gardner's shop, with the same time-won layers. That was what those two had been looking at—not just a horn from some sheep, but a larger pattern and process. An index of the world, of life. In that light, in that moment, it was one thing—the mountains, the ocean floor, and we animals crawling over it all.

8

THE SUBLIME

TWO WEEKS AFTER my time with Don Gardner I was still in his part of the world, staying at the nearby Banff Centre. I'd joined the faculty there and spent my afternoons reading essays or meeting with writers in the miniature cabins they'd been assigned. Occasionally this colony of writers, along with myself and other faculty, would meet in the largest of the cabins to drink coffee in creaking chairs, discuss our craft, and generally indulge our shared anxieties. Mornings, though, I'd rise early to hammer away on an elliptical machine at the gym. I was headed there shortly after sunrise, half-awake and shivering as I bisected a grove at the centre of campus, when a lizard-level alarm in my brain made me freeze among the trees and pull out my earbuds.

A snort to my left. The tilt of a great solemn head. I had walked into a herd of grazing elk, a full dozen of them. I'd seen one on my way to Gardner's workshop, which had been unnerving, but this was paralyzing—a tyranny of elk.

"Whatever you do," a staffer had warned me on arrival, "do not get yourself between a mother elk and her calf. She'll charge." I was currently between three or four mothers and their young, having managed, in my semi-conscious state, to weave myself among them. Now we were all very awake and there was no way to move forward or back. I was suspended in a web of stares, caught by the attention of each seven-hundred-pound creature. I gripped my earbuds to keep the Beyoncé from spilling out.

I was dimly aware of each elk's magnificence—had never seen one, let alone a dozen, this close. But mostly the word *scoot* was honking in my head. As for the elk, they only stared and breathed clouds.

They were eventually forgiving. Sensing my puny-ness, they flicked a few contemptuous ears and walked on, parting around me like bullies who couldn't be bothered. I hurried to the safety of the gym and life went on. But the pleasant mundanity that made up life at the Centre, the murmur of writers and lunchtime talk of Joan Didion, kept getting smashed by these wild moments, glimpses of bears or rolls of summer thunder. Everything in the mountains kept threatening to boulder through, clip my attention. There was a sense that something immense and looming was just beyond, pressurizing the air, something fantastically disinterested in the bit of prose scrawled within my head.

After my time with Gardner I went more often into the woods, wanting to see the world "as it is." But close attention to trees, to trails, to birds and bones, never stopped at the material. Even sitting on a rock to examine a butter-coloured anemone could inspire awe and wonder. Reverence. And I began to see that Craft was not the only thing I'd been missing. There was another blur shaking in the air. Another story I didn't know.

WHEN MY HUSBAND flew in from Vancouver I worried that the feeling would disappear, that his arrival would snap my mind back to our ordinary life, and the shaking space would vanish.

In fact, when Kenny stepped off the bus, laden with bags, he had a handsome grin and was taking big lungfuls of Rocky Mountain air. He was ready, wanted to know this landscape as much as I did. We decided to spend the next day at nearby Lake Louise, one of the turquoise beauties made famous on Canadian postcards.

This was the first sunny Sunday in a month, so the parking spot we found was by a hamlet an hour's hike down the road. (Two million carloads of tourists arrive at Louise each year.)[118] From there, we stumbled across the Bow River and three miles uphill on the gravel shoulder. Thoughts of Don Gardner's twenty-one-day ski trip to Louise silenced my complaints.

The lake is fed by the subarctic Mount Victoria, whose Victoria Glacier falls away in a deadly plunge toward the water's edge. The mountain is a mass of sedimentary rock laid down in shallow seas 500 million years ago, during the Cambrian Period, a seabed that now rests 11,000 feet above sea level. Its icebound peaks melt down sheer cliffs into waterways. What's singular about the effect is how compact mountain, glacier, and lake have become—how each element stacks on the others to create a packed tableau. Visitors feel they've been physically struck. And all the while, the frigid waters flow out, oblivious to our wonder, running eventually through half the breadth of Canada before they pour into Hudson Bay.

The Indigenous Stoney people named the place Ho-Run-Num-Nay, meaning "lake of little fishes." The first British person to arrive was more rapturous, calling it "Emerald Lake." It was then named Louise two years later, to honour Queen Victoria's fourth daughter. By the time Kenny and I arrived it had gathered so much holiness from tourist propaganda that it was hard, at first, to see the scene as real. It was a poster of a landscape, a fantasy. But we hiked one of its branching trails, got a few hundred metres above the lakeshore, found a rocky plinth to sit on far from the crowd, and after some minutes of staring the view shifted away from the picturesque into something more troubling—I found that the mountain, the glacier, were *too* real. They were a pure input that pierced all irony, all distraction, all human shields. I felt, then, like an ophthalmologist's patient who, with dilated eyes, walks suddenly out into sunlight and goes blind.

IT'S TRUE THAT the outdoors may please us, may lower heart rates and cortisol levels, but it is so much more than a bubble bath. The outdoors can ravish and attack, it can bowl us over and dominate the senses. An urbanized humanity forgets how violent, how knock-you-down, the natural world can be. But we remember again in those rare moments when the storm bellows, when the glacier looms, when we encounter the sublime.

Some seek out the sublime in nature as dutifully as church-goers. The poet Samuel Taylor Coleridge used to stand on the edge of cliffs in order to give himself vertigo. The naturalist John Muir would prescribe himself crashing waterfalls. Both sought to provoke in themselves an experience of religious ecstasy, a dose of sublimity. After a trip to France, Coleridge wrote an ode about the relief he felt in a raw encounter with the elements:

> And there I felt thee!—on that sea-cliff's verge,
> Whose pines, scarce travelled by the breeze above,
> Had made one murmur with the distant surge!
> Yes, while I stood and gazed, my temples bare,
> And shot my being through earth, sea, and air,
> Possessing all things with intensest love,
> O Liberty! My spirit felt thee there.[119]

This was not forest bathing. Coleridge had gone and drowned himself. He made a habit of such drownings. A few years later he reported on another alpine reverie in a letter to Sara Hutchinson:

> My limbs were all in a tremble—I lay upon my back to
> rest myself, and was beginning according to my custom
> to laugh at myself for a madman, when the sight of the

crags above me on each side, and the impetuous clouds
just over them, posting so luridly and so rapidly
northward, overawed me. I lay in a state of almost
prophetic trance and delight . . .[120]

These encounters with the sublime, which look in our cyn-
ical times like romantic indulgences, were to the poet vials of
tonic—and they startled readers who thought only churches
could deliver such revelations (and then only during weekly,
organized sessions).

While Coleridge found his medicine in the "sea-cliff's verge"
and among "impetuous clouds," we can of course encounter
the sublime in all kinds of arenas. It might arrive through
philosophical epiphanies, grand literature, or even through
the contemplation of physics—some experience the sublime
while imagining infinity, or trying to comprehend the speed
of light. We can also experience it, paradoxically, in humble
places. A glint of light on a few wet stones might leave you
marvelling at the unimaginable detail of creation. The philosopher Arthur Schopenhauer believed the sublime lives in such
tiny moments, so long as they let us notice a fantastic complexity. The marvels of the universe may be apprehended in a
single leaf. More of us are like Coleridge, though, and find the
sublime in nature's blockbusters. Starry nights can work, or an
expanse of parched desert. When I read that some experience
it by observing herds of animals I thought of the elk at Banff
and wondered if they were a warmup for, an intimation of, my
feelings at Louise.

MICHAEL HARRIS

CHURCHES SOMETIMES ENCOURAGE us to think of the physical world as a shadow of another, eternal reality, but we can also reverse that and see the spiritual as a reflection of the physical world's glory. The greatest painter of the sublime, Caspar David Friedrich, made this explicit when he associated towering evergreen firs with the architecture of cathedrals. He knew that we go to the mountains seeking more than rest and relaxation; we seek answers, a framework for our fragility, a synthesis. We seek a god by another name.

By studying trees and streams we glimpse the laws of the universe. We may even glimpse its very constitution if we look deep enough. Here is the journalist Donovan Webster recalling the moment he rappelled into a live volcano on the archipelago of Vanuatu:

> Acidic gas bites my nose and eyes ... each new breath from the volcano heaves the air so violently my ears pop in the changing pressure—the temperature momentarily soars. Somewhere not too far below, red-hot, pumpkin-size globs of ejected lava are flying through the air ... Yet suspended hundreds of feet above lava up to 2,200 degrees Fahrenheit that reaches toward the centre of the Earth, I'm also discovering there's more. It is stupefyingly beautiful.[121]

In the face of elemental powers we are put, abashedly, in our place. We see that we are *part* of nature and could never be its master. Consumer culture argues just the opposite: You are not *part* of nature; rather, you hold dominion over it. The volcano would not dare swallow you.

When we fill our days with buying and selling we come to believe that our role on the planet is to plunder, to invade and take; we come to believe we are "personalities" primed for self-promotion and comfort, separate from the world's own mysterious work. This divorce between people and the planet was anticipated by Karl Marx in his magnum opus *Das Kapital*, where he writes that capitalist production disturbs "the metabolic interaction between man and earth."[122] He was thinking in surprisingly literal terms, about the nutrients we derive from the earth and the manure we excrete back into it. The urbanity that capitalism makes possible removes us from the countryside and thus makes us into thieves, pulling in nature's nutrients without returning any fertilizer to the farmed land. Marx saw that overworked soil was the result and that we'd turn to artificial fertilizers to push nature beyond its limits. So, while Marx is famous for describing how capitalism undermines the worker, he also saw that it undermines our other source of wealth, the supporting landscape. And his interest in exhausted soil anticipated a hundred further exhaustions, in the sea, in the sky, in the hearts of rocky quarries—a hundred bad bargains and unjust deals that capitalism tries to force upon the Earth. There are many contradictions inherent to capitalism, but this robbing of nature for short-term gain is the stupidest. The fact that our lives really do play out in precise concert with systems of plant, animal, mineral, and gas is brushed to one side, forgotten, and, in place of that fact, we have egos and advertisements, our two most beloved abstractions.

Consumer culture keeps pretending that we've somehow done away with nature. We affect disconnection. Today's children spend half as much time playing outside as their parents did;[123] adults spend at least 90 percent of their lives indoors.[124] A "nature-deficit disorder"[125] brings on "sky blindness" and "plant blindness"[126] until nature itself becomes a shady unknown and we're turned into existential orphans, unaware of our own green origins.

In reality, it is the planet that can afford to not know us. Without us, the Earth would thrive. In the Korean Demilitarized Zone, for example, a stretch of land 155 miles long and 1.5 miles wide was ceded back to nature following the armistice between North and South in 1953—and rice paddies that were maintained for centuries swiftly reverted to marsh. Were humans to disappear all over the planet, the proof of our civilizations' existence would not fare better. In a matter of centuries, genetically modified crops would be wiped out; skyscrapers would be toppled by water freezing in cracks and the inexorable progress of tree roots; sewers would clog and roads would buckle; my hometown would become a forest of cedar and fir; even our loving dogs, paragons of a tamed wild, would first go feral and then be replaced entirely by other carnivores.[127]

The mountains, the oceans, the ozone layer, were never sculpted for our enjoyment, our casual use. This is what the sublime can teach. That we are, despite the obsessiveness of our daily strategies and exploits, tethered to something magnificent and grand—not a god, but a planet.

IN THE MIDDLE of the eighteenth century, as a mania for nature worship took hold among poets and philosophers, a young man from Dublin was bothered by it all. Edmund Burke wanted to know why people should be drawn toward scenes of crashing waterfalls and roaring storms. Safeguarding one's life was surely the highest good, and these dalliances with danger didn't make much sense. So, in a brief period between university and his career as a statesman, Burke wrote a heartfelt and weird little book called *A Philosophical Enquiry Into the Sublime and Beautiful.*

Burke began by making a crucial distinction between beautiful things and sublime things. "Beautiful," as a category, was fairly easy to understand; we love the beautiful, he supposed, because it signifies safety, health, and good order. The symphonies of Mozart, the paintings of Rembrandt—these please us because they lend a sense of mastery to our ears and eyes. Our attraction toward the sublime, though, was harder to explain. Sublime things were overpowering and humans generally hate to be overpowered, so why should we sometimes *like* it? There had to be a psychological or spiritual benefit to witnessing the bigness and indifference of the universe—and, consequently, a benefit to embracing our own insignificance.

One proposition: the enormity of sublime things can put our little worries into context, can make human troubles appear inconsequential. In other words, when the sublime diminishes us it can't help but diminish our worries, too. All the trappings of consumer culture, for example, begin to look pointless. Our worldly goods are made ridiculous when placed on snowy Alps or plunked into infinite seascapes. The sublime pops overinflated egos and reminds us to not put too much weight in our daily scrounging for fine clothes and overpriced wine.

This is a healthy self-negation, a healthy humility, and one that's become more profound in the twenty-first century. Even while we are encouraged by product-hawkers to think of ourselves as a "brand called You," our scientists place us in a more and more obscure and humble position with each new breakthrough. The farther their telescopes peer into the universe, the smaller and more backward our corner of space appears. Even if we ignore the cold shoulder the heavens offer and focus on planet Earth, we have to admit that humans are only bit players, newly arrived on the stage of a 4.5-billion-year-old play starring fungal colonies and brachiopods. And, to the grandeur Burke found in the Earth's crackling crust, we can add our knowledge that the continents under our feet are always moving at the same speed our fingernails grow, that the continental outlines we memorized in childhood are only temporary forms. The Earth is even now sliding past our conception of it, into new shapes with new mountains and oceans. We know, in a way Burke could only intuit, that forces infinitely larger than us will reshape all the homelands we imagine to be solid and unchanging. We know that, one day, continents currently separated by an ocean will meet again, ram together, and form a new Alps where today there is bottomless water. We know that fields of marine snow that have covered ocean floors for millions of years will one day rest in mountain valleys, and real snow will then blanket those trillions of buried plankton.

We can even humble ourselves by looking straight inside our bodies to see how little of what we find there can be called our own. Human cells only make up 43 percent of the cells in your body—the others are bacteria, viruses, fungi, and archaea, all hitching a ride on a human-shaped spaceship.[128] We could not survive without this alien microbiome any more than we could survive without the trees and animals and planet-sized systems operating outside our bodies (and, what's more, the two biomes are synergistic). It has become nearly impossible to *not* sense how interdependent, contingent, and partial we really are. Knowing all this—glimpsing our sublime reality—could set us up for a new relationship with the environment. We should be more awed and humbled by our view than Coleridge and Burke were awed and humbled by theirs.

BUT THE COUNTERVAILING instinct—to lord over the land—runs deep. Almost a century before Burke inquired into the value of sublime landscapes, theologian Thomas Burnet saw in mountains nothing but nuisance. In his 1681 book *Telluris Theoria Sacra* ("The Sacred Theory of the Earth") Burnet proposed that our planet had originally been shaped by the Creator as a "mundane egg" with "not a wrinkle, scar or fracture in all its body; no rocks, nor mountains, no hollow caves, nor gaping channels, but even and uniform all over."[129] This imagined mundanity was even reflected in the Earth's original skies:

And the smoothness of the earth made the face of the heavens so too; the air was calm and serene; none of

those tumultuary motions and conflicts of vapours,
which the mountains and the winds cause in ours: it
was suited to a golden Age, and to the first innocency
of nature.[130]

A perfect creation, perfectly smooth. The vast irruptions of mountains that we now live with must, in fact, be evidence of some terrible error that took place after Creation; they must be disruptions that occurred in the time of Noah's flood. (Burnet archly points out that mountains are never mentioned in Genesis.) The vision is profound and ridiculous and belligerent, with its suggestion that life on Earth is not *meant* to include disruptions, that humans *ought* to be roaming a smooth and forgiving landscape with no hurdles in our path. It's golden-age thinking, blithe and grabby. It assumes we'd have the run of the place if only Satan hadn't messed things up. Another Burnet—Gilbert Burnet, the bishop of Salisbury—read the first Burnet's book, travelled through the Alps himself, and wrote home to concur with his namesake:

When one considers the Height of these Hills, the Chain
of so many of them together, and their Extent both in
Length and Breadth . . . these cannot be the Primary
Productions of the Author of Nature but are the vast
Ruines of the first World, which at the Deluge broke here
into so many Inequalities.[131]

Where lovers of the sublime learn from mountains how small and fragile we are, the Burnets of the world refuse that lesson, preferring to imagine that the world as it is—rough, broken, crushing—is one big mistake. Today, 340 years after *Telluris Theoria Sacra*, those who deny climate change cling to the Burnet-ian vision: they suppose the world was made to accommodate human wishes; and when scientists say we cannot do with it what we will, Team Burnet fantasizes about that "mundane egg" whose yolk is theirs to fry.

From seventeenth-century theologians to twenty-first-century oil magnates, the hope remains that humans are *not* small, that we are kings of creation. And we each avoid that feeling of insignificance every time we find solace in consumer culture. For what is a trip to the mall if not an assertion that the universe is clean, controllable, and designed for our pleasure? We enter a world unto itself, bright and manufactured, with its own recycled atmosphere, its own waterworks and potted nature, a world sanitized, bagged, and crying *please own me*. Instead of being squashed by the raw elements, instead of dangling over lava, we insulate ourselves with shopping. And it's no surprise that shopping addicts often focus on clothing, the armour of mall-based selfhood.[132] We can draw a direct line from Burnet's impossibly smooth Earth, through the climate-denier's consumption of oil fields, to a shopaholic's desperate visits to the mall. It is all one denial of the lesson that the sublime seeks to teach us. The urge to "leave with something" is the opposite of the urge that Burke or Coleridge or Muir were following; when they went to the cliff's edge, the waterfall's cusp, they were looking to be stripped.

ENCOUNTERS WITH THE sublime can do more than just humble us, though. They can also raise us up. The sublime can open a liminal space where the individual and the transcendent briefly merge. So: by comprehending the glory of the Grand Canyon, my mind expands to encompass its vast dimensions. "We experience a type of mental 'swelling,'" says Professor Linda Marie Brooks, "expanding, as it were, to meet and embrace a part of the object's power."[133] By looking hard into the heart of a tidal wave, a cliff face, the Milky Way, we face up to its threat and match it with our comprehension. In the moment when we realize the world is greater than we ever supposed, we are also amazed to find that our ability to *perceive* that greatness is, itself, greater than we ever supposed. This is not simply a thrill; it's a profoundly *useful* education. Real insights are glimpsed, not via rational arguments but through an aesthetic reordering, a breakdown of our faculties that leaves us open to perceiving something new.

Cuban poet José María Heredia felt that psychic rupture when he saw Niagara Falls:

You flow serene, majestic, and then
crashing onto sharp rugged rocks,
violently you dash forward, relentless
like destiny, irresistible and blind.
What human voice could describe
the terrifying spectacle,
reflecting on the seething current
that my clouded vision vainly tries
to follow as it sweeps to the wide edge

of so high a cliff. A thousand waves,
moving rapidly like thoughts,
clash in wild fury;
another thousand, and yet another rush to join them,
and amid foam and clamour they disappear.[134]

Heredia sees in the falls a power beyond his words ("What human voice could describe . . ."), beyond his sight ("my clouded vision vainly tries . . ."), and beyond his understanding (later he writes, "My mind is lost . . ."). The poet gains access to an *intimation* of greatness. He cries out: "Vain ravings! / Oh! I am banished, / without homeland, without love . . ." This is the sublime as reckoner, as revealer of our reality's grand design. Albert Einstein felt we should seek to be thrown over in this way if we want brave new ideas. "The most beautiful thing we can experience is the mysterious," he wrote. "It is the source of all true art and science. He to whom the emotion is a stranger, who can no longer pause to wonder and stand wrapped in awe, is as good as dead; his eyes are closed."[135] The sublime is a teacher that unsettles, one that turns over the tidy desk.

Knowing that our minds cannot fully comprehend the totality of things—becoming acquainted, in other words, with the colossal majesty of existence—is, for Einstein, "the centre of true religiousness."[136] His kind of religion inspires an inquiry, a habit of being curious about this universe's arrangements (not unlike Don Gardner's habitual workshop curiosity). Such an appetite for the sublime was a prerequisite for discovering that moving clocks are slower than stationary clocks, or that energy and mass are perfectly convertible. What better attitude is there than awe when we set out to learn?

HIGHER, HIGHER. WE climbed past Lake Louise, through mud chopped rough by trail horses, to a smaller, isolated lake of fainter emerald, perched far above and circled by its own swooping mountainscape. These peaks bore snowy cornices and were iced in their crevices so that shadows became anti-shadows, shining white. We stripped down to T-shirts and bathed in the chilled air.

Soon the mud was gone and we were scrambling over dry grey rock. Trees grew sparse, the lake's water moved from jewel tones to stewed spinach whenever a cloud skidded overhead. A clay was packed into the mountain's lower folds and fanned out into the water's edge. This was the silt, the constant feed of rock flour that's ground high up where ice scrapes stone and moves—through avalanche or crumb-by-crumb inching—toward the water. It's these travelling grains that become suspended in the lake and, by reflecting sunlight, do their tiny part to turn the water green. At the lakeshore we were both above and below all this, two small witnesses to a colossal process.

We were unprepared, giddy, at finding ourselves so near a magic larger and older than anything we knew in our city lives. The floating green dust seemed, suddenly, like an after-image of the trillions of plankton that shower the ocean floor—and a febrile tremor traced my brain. Kenny shouted at nothing. I shouted. The air was a cold magnificence and a ground

squirrel emerged from his rocky warren to rear a few trium-
phant inches onto hind legs and bark.

MONTHS LATER, I tried to label the feeling. First I spoke
with "neuro-aesthetics" researchers who study fMRI brain
scans while subjects observe sublime landscapes; little was
gained. Beyond goosebumps, "chills," and a change of heart-
rate, hardly anything is known about the physical mechanisms
that underlie our experience of the sublime. Some say it is
the mind's attempt to embrace and accommodate something
so vast that it causes cognitive realignment. Some say it is the
mind witnessing its own inability to take things in. But the
gears and clockwork of the sublime remain a mystery.

The evolutionary point of our chills is guessed at too.
Perhaps we evolved a sense of awe in order to adhere us to a
single leader when primate groups expanded. Perhaps it gave
us a sense of external greatness that tamped down selfish
behaviour, promoted social cohesion. There must, we assume,
be some practical point to the shivering *glory* of things. But
perhaps there is none at all, perhaps it's an accidental leftover
of our mind's development, like some vestigial organ.

I spoke with psychologist Matthew Pelowski at the University of Vienna, and he was more helpful because he largely
ignored the sublime's murky origins and described instead its
effects—the way it produces very real mental shifts:

It's beyond the faculties we have. But at some point you
find a way of dealing with that. You realize, "I have the

faculty to appreciate the fact that this is beyond me." It matches the psychological process for how we grow or change our ideas, learn new things.

Pelowski described a profound humility—a humility like Einstein's—that jump-starts curiosity in turn. A neurobiologist I later spoke with seemed to echo this idea; he'd found that parts of the brain connected with self-awareness are deactivated during intense experiences of the sublime.[137] Subjects simply lost their egos in the presence of awesome sights. And all this dovetailed with what the philosophers had said as well. A dose of the sublime could wrench us free from our stubborn patterns, our stubborn selves.

Still, none of that analysis can fully explain the feeling itself—the expansive moment of de-personhood, re-personhood, obliteration and consolidation, that we get from staring into the pearlescence of the northern lights—the pulsing, reverent *almost contact* I felt crawling in a mountain's titanic shadow, where glacier-ground rock dust was turning, through an alchemy older than recorded history, a clear lake into liquid emerald.

SO LONG AS we stayed there in the wild, Kenny and I were free from our worries. Back home in Vancouver we'd been wrestling for months with the privileged drama of buying a condo. And now, on the mountainside, we were cut loose from a list I'd made of all the new furniture we needed, loose from the spreadsheets Kenny was building in anticipation of a months-long renovation of the new place's falling-apart kitchen, its mouldering cabinets. It made a deep kind of sense to just stay there by the lake, away from all that neurotic domestic struggle—stay a year or ten at the water's edge and let that life fall apart, explode if it wanted. Something seemed to be bursting; I felt like a pipe when the water freezes. All those old anxieties were nothing, or were nothing in that one moment. "Do you think we can get over there?" I asked suddenly, a little desperate, pointing to the far shore where an avalanche had skirted the mountain with gravel. But there was no way; the landscape grew violent and impossible the farther we hiked. We had no idea how to continue. Don Gardner had told me he'd traversed every one of these peaks; and here we were, unable to scramble up one pebbly fringe. Eventually we turned to stumble back down the mountain.

I feared, again, that the feeling would go, that my experience of the sublime would be superficial and leave me unchanged. I feared being unchanged because change was so clearly necessary. In the revelling, in the sublime, you see something so obvious and crucial to human survival—our dependence. Your life is shaken and your view of things painfully expands, stretches to terrifying dimensions. And you realize—out in the woods, up the mountain, inside the pocket of a wave— that nature is not something we visit, and certainly not something we own; it is something we are. We have somehow been given the ability to tremble with an apprehension that we are the Marble Caves of Chile; the moon-like deserts of Egypt; the Monteverde Cloud Forest of Costa Rica, the Mauna Loa volcano in Hawaii; and every breathing creature, too. We have the fleeting ability to sense all that in a wash of egoless awe. It is a glimpse of how it would feel to love the planet as we love ourselves.

KENNY LEFT FOR Vancouver the morning after our hike. Two hours driving down, out of the Rockies, to catch his flight at the Calgary airport. Work was calling. Life. And also tragedy, though I didn't know that yet.

9

CARE

KENNY SAT NEAR me on the sofa and stared at a corner of the floor. His shoulders began to round and I asked how things had gone.

"You know those horror movies," he said, "where the big bad takes on the shape of someone you love? And you know they aren't really the person, not the person you care about, but they have that person's body? And so you still reach out, even though it's a trick? It's sometimes—it's sometimes like that."

EARLIER THAT YEAR we were walking in a long, deviating oval around Trout Lake on the east side of Vancouver, and Kenny said, "I think there's something wrong with Omma." He sped up.

"Wrong how?" I hurried to keep pace.

Kenny chewed his lip, squinted down at our dog padding between us. It was a gorgeous day and there were dogs everywhere, chasing, yawping.

"Did she say something?" I asked.

"No. But you know how she's been calling. A lot."

I did know. Sometimes we woke to a dozen missed calls from Kenny's mom. The week before, they'd made lunch plans, confirmed the location twice, and she still wound up waiting at the wrong restaurant. This lost quality of hers had been coming on so slowly, though, that it seemed halfway natural. Then again, my take didn't count for much because, to me, Kenny's mom was always a little obscured by a language barrier—her English was rudimentary and my Korean non-existent.

"Well, what are we talking about?" I asked Kenny as we turned off the path, onto the lakeshore. "Do you mean something mental? Like you think she's got dementia?" It was so easy, then, to throw out words like that. They had no reality to them, they referred to an imaginary crisis you read about in newspapers, saying, "just awful; must be hell." Something that dragged down a group of poor others.

Broaching the subject that day seemed to unleash her symptoms, like an incantation or jinx. Soon confusions and paranoias broke through the surface of her demeanour and it became impossible to deny that something had fallen apart in her mind. Omma began complaining about a woman who lived in the bathroom mirror and emerged to steal her things. To thwart this thief she would hide her favourite clothes in stashes around the apartment. She then forgot where she'd hidden them, or that she'd hidden them at all, and so her original delusion became a self-fulfilling prophecy—the woman in the mirror, who was herself, was indeed stealing her things.

Kenny's father took an old shower curtain and duct-taped it over the mirror. But this only bounced the confusion from one pane of glass to others: soon Omma's computer and phone became portals for her fantasies. She watched YouTube videos of Korean pop stars like Patti Kim and Moon Ju-Ran, insisting the celebrities were her intimate friends. She carried on conversations with the singers through the glass. When Kenny came to visit she would sit him down and introduce her son to these famous friends, all of whom agreed: Omma had a beautiful singing voice. In fact, she would sing for them when they asked, conjuring hundreds of audience members in her two-bedroom apartment. The audience would disappear just as Kenny arrived.

We moved Omma and Appa into a retirement home that offered far less care than Omma required. A place where meals were provided and weekly laundry was handled but which could not manage the scope of her deteriorating condition. The new apartment had a small kitchen and bedroom, a living room with a TV, all the makings of a miniature home, and placing them there allowed us to fool ourselves a little longer into believing things could continue apace, that a life, a mind, was not disassembling before us. We bought a full set of flat-packed IKEA furniture and spent a day building it, imagining a comfortable life for his parents. I still had in my head a simple idea of dementia and dementia's care, where Omma would sit quietly at a window, perhaps work on a puzzle or flip contentedly through a picture book. I kept saying we should buy Time-Life volumes from the 1960s and 70s, books full of images that might jog her memory.

Kenny and I went to clear out the downtown apartment where his parents had lived for decades. By the kitchen faucet a fledgling bit of ivy grew from a jar of water, its raw roots feeling the edge of the glass. In the sink lay a set of commemorative forks that Omma would bring out with platters of sliced fruit. On the fridge were cheerful remnants from her magnet collection—Hawaiian sunsets and smiley faces. In the living room hunkered a bizarrely large tangle of wires, big as an eagle's nest; vines crawled out of baskets and a stuffed monkey hid among them. In the bedroom I found another nest, this one made of neckties, dozens of them knotted on the closet floor. A journal beneath the bed held poetry written in Korean and (in one of Omma's constant efforts at language learning) studiously translated into English below. Flipping through, I read: "We have no cry to predict our future. We can live for today." And everywhere: Scrabble tiles; coat hangers; all the loose ends and frayed bits. Under the sink and in the closets, dozens of bottles of unopened cleaners. Down windows I wiped paper towels that came away black.

After cleaning their old place I saw that we'd wandered toward another blur, a space in our lives that needed another new story to bring it meaning. We would spend years writing that one.

I AM TOLD that someone on the planet develops dementia every three seconds.[138] But what can that possibly mean?

Dementia is not a lamp switching off. It is the evening sun, moving by degrees so imperceptible we cannot say when things are halfway gone, or when they have disappeared altogether. It darkens, eats at, the corners of experience, first seeming like a trick of our perceptions, but proceeding inexorably until at last we find ourselves swept past the warning stage and mired in the irrefutable night. And yet there must have been some three-second period, I suppose, when one could say, "Now she has lost herself. Now we have lost her."

There were many false returns to her former self before that final disappearance. The path would waver, double back on itself before returning to its downward arc. I asked Kenny, "When was the last time you felt like your mom was taking care of you?" And he remembered a moment just before we moved his parents and cleaned out their old apartment, a moment when he was fighting with his father about her. They had begun discussing her condition in her presence, since she couldn't follow their English anyhow. Reading their emotions, though, Omma came between them and told Kenny's father to stop upsetting her son. Bewildered, she insisted that Kenny should not be worried. "It was this little bit of script," he told me. "Somehow, through all the tangles and plaques in the brain, some little script about protecting me got triggered. And that was—well, the last time she acted like my mom."

THERE IS AN enormous difference between the adulthood that consumer culture promised and the one we inevitably inherit. Consumer culture promised a future of agency, a state of powerful arrival, an experience of control over our circumstances and even control over the way we feel. But real life, when it mows over you, leaves nearly the opposite impression: it makes you into an adult by forcing you to see you have no control; life reveals itself to be a nearly comical battle against entropy. We learn there is no single beautiful story awaiting our recitation, that instead there are many half-broken and tender ideas of a story, each needful and necessary but fallible in its own way. And nowhere is this truth more evident than in the years we spend caring for our parents.

Kenny and I have parents at the oldest edge of the Baby Boom, which means we are harbingers of a sort. Our experience is common enough already, but care for a parent with dementia is about to define a generation. Such care will explode in our lifetimes, will dominate the millennial's attention, the millennial's bank account, and—most painfully—the millennial's conscience. Only climate change—another reckoning with our ability to care—will rival it.

As Omma's illness became obvious, she joined fifty million other dementia sufferers around the globe. That number will more than triple over the next few decades, rising to 152 million by 2050.[139] (The global senior citizen population is, itself, ballooning.)[140] The global cost of caring for all those dementia patients will double, from its current position at $1 trillion each year to $2 trillion. Meanwhile, a shortage of geriatric caretakers is also imminent.[141] (Building that army of specialized caretakers is especially difficult because geriatricians are not especially well paid; they earn half as much as radiologists and cardiologists.)[142] And all this is only the beginning of our potential burden. In poorer countries like India, for example, 90 percent of all dementia cases go undiagnosed.[143] If all the world became as privileged as America, diagnoses—and costs—would skyrocket.

Of course, even those trillions of dollars are only a mitigation, a fractional help. The lived reality is still chaos, still heartache. In the spring, only a few weeks after we moved Kenny's parents to their retirement home, we got a call from his father, who had been pushed past his breaking point. Omma had kept him up all night—again—yelling at him, raving. She pulled a knife.

The previous day they'd been to her psychiatrist, who warned that she must be admitted to a psych ward if these new aggressive spells continued. And so Kenny and I drove over, packed them into the backseat, and brought them to Mount Saint Joseph Hospital. A strangely simple act in the moment—as though we were all going out to dinner or on a slightly tedious errand. After Kenny buckled his mother in she simply stared out the window; it had been months since she'd asked where she was being taken.

The only way into the psych ward at Mount Saint Joseph is through the Emergency room, so we trundled in and began a half day of intake interviews and tests. A nurse applied sensors to Omma's chest for readings and, when she took them off a little roughly, Omma cried out in what seemed a theatrical display of pain. In fact, as she was changed into a hospital gown and forced to wait for hours amidst the ER's chaos, every point of pressure or agitation became outsized, every discomfort an opening for pleas to go home or to be left alone. A psychiatrist came by, a gentle Patch Adams figure in his fifties who talked to Omma as though she were a child. Kenny noticed how effective this was, though it startled him, too. The psychiatrist asked Kenny whether Omma stumbled when she walked, whether she shuffled in place. He was trying to decide between two diagnoses, Alzheimer's or Lewy body dementia—semi-meaningless labels, as it turns out. Naming her illness was a problem that would persist through countless caretakers and multiple institutions. The search for a name, for a tidy category into which we might herd her collection of symptoms, was a search that felt powerfully important at first but then grew wearisome, more meaningless, as the days and weeks wore on. In fact, with or without a name, there were almost no real details about what Omma was going through. We were stunned to learn how nebulous, how shoulder-shrugging, dementia diagnoses can be. Despite those more than fifty million people living with some form of this disease, there is no practical way to diagnose its most common form, Alzheimer's, until a pathologist can look at the deceased patient's brain. And so treatment proceeds by guesses, by inference, by waiting and seeing. Things are thrown at the wall: drugs are tried, combined, doses increased, decreased, all in an effort to hit a constantly moving target that may or may not exist.

At last Omma was laid on a gurney and taken upstairs to the psych ward where she would spend the next several months. That first night, separation—from her husband, from her son—was nearly impossible. She shouted and reached for them, uncomprehending as nurses led her away. Kenny had taken the nurses aside and explained her love for old Korean pop stars, the only distraction he could imagine. And so those nurses sat with her for hours after she'd been left there, into the night, listening—without understanding—to songs from her youth.

Back at our condo, Kenny looked at me and I thought he might vomit from guilt.

OMMA STAYED IN the psych ward for three or four months and then, when a bed became available in a long-term facility, we experienced another flush of naive hope that things could be improved. When Kenny and Omma arrived, though, there was nobody at the entrance to greet them, no proper intake process at all. Omma was assigned a room with a roommate— a paranoid woman who only spoke Chinese, and with whom Omma would now spend weeks in anxious, meaningless debate. (They each were sure the other was stealing.)

When Kenny first left her there, the nurses led Omma down a hall and Kenny went behind a pair of code-locked doors with safety-glass windows. As he stood waiting for the ponderous elevator, Omma fought the nurses off and ran to the door; pounding on the glass square with both fists, she shouted, "Kenny! *Gajima*, Kenny! *Gajima*!" *Don't go! Don't go!*

He pretended not to hear her, and the nurses rushed to pull his mother away again. The elevator arrived and Kenny left. This would more or less be what saying goodbye looked like for months.

We developed a kind of routine where Kenny would visit Omma after work while I made dinner. We'd eat on the sofa and take stabs at discussing what was happening. I felt, during these conversations, as though I could only get hold of the start or end of sentences, that words were failing me so that I babbled or murmured without saying anything helpful. And then, at other times, my words became too precise, too scripted, as though I were reciting a condolence I'd learned from a movie. And, just as I was never saying what I meant exactly, I also wasn't hearing what Kenny meant, either—I listened to the edge of what he told me, afraid to let destruction, and the consequences for the man I loved, sink in.

There was never a time when speaking felt appropriate. It would usually end, anyhow, with more tears and ultimately silence. I sometimes thought, then, how pitiful we must look, if anyone were to glance up from the street into our condo's living room window and see us with bowed heads. But of course I also knew that nobody was going to pity us—because we were, absurdly, grown-ups now.

IF YOU GO looking for it, you will discover a Darwinian theory that suggests humans care for the elderly because grandparents increase the survival rate of their grandchildren and are therefore worth keeping around. This is an odd theory for Kenny and me to contemplate. We are childless and have no need for babysitters. What's more, Omma cannot remember that her two daughters, Kenny's sisters, have brought five grandchildren into her life. Such crude accounting jobs would discover only deficits for those who care for people with dementia. Patients grow selfish, grow child-like, and cannot fathom needs beyond their own. Nor can they fathom the expense (emotional, physical, financial) they incur for those who do the caring.

And so there has always been—alongside a primal need to care for our parents—a fantasy, dark and immensely shameful: *Could I walk away?* Kenny and I do, in fact, walk away, every time we leave her in the care of professionals. We go to dinners, we do our jobs, we do laundry, pretend things are as they were, all while Omma wanders hallways, searching. But there is, for every caretaker, an even darker potential beyond those daily goodbyes at the code-locked door. There is the possibility—seemingly unfathomable but people do it every day—of walking away for good.

The fantasy appears in cultures around the globe. In Japan, a mythical practice of abandoning old men and women on wooded mountains is called *Ubasute.* In Nordic folklore, the elderly are simply thrown over the edge of the most convenient cliff, a grimmer but more efficient end. Shelves of science fiction describe societies where the old and infirm are cut loose in a collective abdication of care that returns trillions of dollars to a grateful state. Everyone over the age of twenty-one is deemed dead weight in the novel *Logan's Run.* (On your twenty-first birthday a crystal implanted in your palm blinks black, reminding you to report to a "Sleepshop" for execution.) This extreme youth bias was a little easier to imagine in the 1960s, when *Logan's Run* was written; the median age in the States was then only twenty-eight[144]—a full decade younger than it is today.[145] *Logan's Run* was written in a world where youths were going to rework society to their own ends. Those youths, of course, are the same people now entering geriatric care centres. As of this writing, the novel's co-authors are ninety-one and eighty-six years old.

Fantasies of senicide, like all fantasies, gain traction in times of extremity. In ancient Germany, the Heruli tribe reportedly could not afford to keep their seniors around and would therefore stab them to death before burning their bodies on pyres. During past famines the Inuit are said to have sometimes left their old on the ice to die of exposure. And then there are more awkward, piecemeal betrayals: the American College of Emergency Physicians reported in 1992 that seventy thousand elderly people had that year been simply abandoned by their families in cases of so-called granny dumping[146] (often in hospital emergency rooms like the one we took Omma to, apologetic notes pinned to their clothing). When *The New York Times* reported on this phenomenon, they found that "when the illness is Alzheimer's, care-givers often veer from despair to burnout."[147] And I don't know how much to blame those granny dumpers and how much to pity them. Certainly each time Kenny leaves his mother, and she pleads with him, and the nurses drag her away, and he pretends not to hear her screams, he has to have a small argument inside his head, has to decide again whether he is a monster or not.

CARE IN EXTREMITY makes us question our humanity because it forces us to confront our interdependence in ways that consumer culture does not. It makes us remember what we always were—animals profoundly attentive to each other's needs.

The primatologist Frans de Waal highlights the care primates live by in his observation of Kidogo, an adult bonobo with a heart condition that left him weak and mentally infirm. When Kidogo was brought to the Milwaukee County Zoo he became lost and could not follow instructions from zookeepers. The other bonobos in the enclosure recognized their new member's predicament and began taking him by the hand and leading him wherever the zookeepers wanted him to go. "They understood both the keepers' intentions and Kidogo's problem," reports de Waal. "Soon Kidogo began to rely on their help. If he felt lost, he would utter distress calls, and others would quickly come over to calm him and act as a guide."[148] It's often assumed that such care is the natural province of low-rung members of society, an inglorious duty offloaded to those who cannot hunt or exert authority, so it's instructive to discover that one of Kidogo's most constant helpers was Lody, the group's alpha male.[149] Lody carried Kidogo around when he could no longer move on his own and even hand-fed Kidogo the choicest pieces of food. Here was a powerful leader who felt caring for the weak was a crucial part of his role. On other occasions Lody would lead a blind, elderly female from place to place, and even adopted orphaned infants, cradling them in his arms.[150] Such care is the hallmark of heroes, not servants. And theirs is a heroics of the everyday.

When we take the time to really observe animals, stories like this—stories of the thoughtful, elaborate care often imagined to be a strictly human attribute—show up everywhere.

Such care even crosses species barriers: a bear adopts a tiger into its family; bottlenose dolphins surround a human swimmer to defend him from an attacking shark; an elephant pulls out gate locks to release a herd of captive antelope. These stories make me think that when Kenny first reached for his confused mother's hand he was enacting something that's ancient and integral not just to mothers, or children, or even the human race, but to the animal kingdom. "Why should our nastiness be the baggage of an apish past and our kindness uniquely human?" asked the paleontologist Stephen Jay Gould. "Why should we not seek continuity with other animals for our 'noble' traits as well?"[151] When we take care of each other we shouldn't say that we're acting like angels; we should say that we're acting like animals. We are becoming our better selves.

THE ROOT OF our instinct to care for each other is more likely a messy *network* of roots, and different specialists will direct you to their favourite offshoot . . .

The neurologist may tell you about "mirror neurons." These were discovered in the early 1990s when a team of researchers at the University of Parma, in Italy, implanted sensors in the brains of macaque monkeys in order to watch their motor systems light up as they grabbed at bananas and other objects. The researchers were stunned to discover that the same neurons were firing whether a monkey picked up a banana or merely watched as one of the researchers did. A graduate student came back from lunch with an ice cream cone and the monkey's brain lit up as though it were holding an ice cream cone of its own. It took years for the lead researcher, Giacomo Rizzolatti, to believe his own results[152] but eventually he concluded that primates have some neurons that are designed to recite, to re-enact, the actions we observe; an elegant way for the mind to understand the motivations of others. Useful, too: if I understand your intentions I am more able to manipulate them. Creatures survive or perish by their ability to deeply understand the actions of others, and mirror neurons may be an evolutionary advantage that promotes this involuntary empathy. They cause some of our most unconscious reactions: if you are shown a smiling or frowning face for even a split second, for instance, you will unwittingly imitate that expression.[153] If another person (or even your dog) yawns in your direction, "yawn contagion" will have you yawning, too. (Autistic children, who often have trouble reading the emotions of others, may exhibit less yawn contagion than non-autistic children.)[154] Other emotional contagions include crying at weddings and dancing at parties. We're hardwired to share and reflect the states we witness in those around us. This has concrete benefits in the wild. Yawn contagion, for example, allows groups of apes to coordinate their sleep patterns. And a flock of resting birds will suddenly alight en masse to synchronize an escape from a predator that only one bird has noticed.[155]

The neurologist's mirror neurons and contagious moods are only one of care's possible roots, though. The psychologist may prefer to explain the instinct to care by telling you about "theory of mind," our ability to understand that other people are, in fact, other people. We each begin life by knowing only our own minds, and then develop the superpower of divining

some of us don't...

other people's perspectives. Babies are not born with theory of mind and seem to assume that the universe is a lonely kingdom, an enormous extension of their tiny will. Mirror neurons may fire in an infant primate's brain—inspiring it to imitate facial gestures, for example—but theory of mind is less automatic and takes years to develop. (Work begins early, though; children as young as one can recognize the distress of a family member and may even attempt to console them.)[156] As we grow up, we each develop this theory for ourselves, discovering that other humans are not merely a supporting cast in the drama of our lives but individuals with complicated interior selves that can often come into conflict with our own. It remains a "theory," however, because the minds of others do remain secret, unknowable, even while we assume they are there. As with mirror neurons, this act of perspective-taking has obvious advantages: if I'm able to think about your intentions as separate from my own, I may be able to manipulate you, or strategize ways to capture your resources. At the same time, perspective-taking opens the door to empathic feelings. Most of us end up compulsively considering the feelings of others. We do it automatically, and so indiscriminately that we'll even take seriously the feelings of fictional characters in a novel or movie. So developed is our theory of mind that we spin other selves into being without really trying.

A third explanation for our instinct to care comes from biologists who talk about "biological altruism." A bumblebee sacrifices itself to defend the hive; a vampire bat regurgitates blood into the mouth of a neighbour bat whose hunt was unsuccessful; a sterile ant devotes its entire life to the well-being of a colony despite having no chance of producing offspring; a blackbird spots a hawk and lets out a warning call, benefitting other birds while drawing dangerous attention to itself. Nature is filled with examples of creatures who give up some part of their own "fitness" to support the fitness of others. Darwin's concept of natural selection, though, suggests that our actions are always, ultimately, designed to ensure that we pass genes on to offspring. So what would explain the instinct to support those who aren't our children? For biologists, the mystery is solved when we consider that the law of evolution is enforced not just at an individual level but at the group level, as well. Selfish and nepotistic genes may have evolved to ensure that John Smith keeps himself strong, passes his genes on to his children, and then protects those children as they mature; but, at the same time, altruistic genes have evolved to ensure that the larger community will thrive. A group of primates com-posed of purely selfish beings would fare very poorly com-pared to one that shared resources, warned each other about predators, and cared for the sick. Members of altruistic groups therefore pass on their altruistic genes even if such genes only benefit the group as a whole—even if they sometimes *hurt* the survival chances of an individual. Darwin himself seems to propose this concept of "group selection" a dozen years after *On the Origin of Species* in his 1871 book *The Descent of Man.* A century later, Richard Dawkins would detail in *The Selfish Gene* how it really is the survival of this gene or that one—the *data* of life—that is the driving force of evolution, and less so the lives of individuals. Being kind, being generous, being altruistic, even taking care of those who can never repay the favour—our genes allow those traits to thrive over the longer arc of history.

The philosopher Peter Singer argues that our civilization has been defined by these caring characteristics.[157] He imagines an ongoing expansion of the circle of people we're able to care about. A primal spark of care between mother and child develops into care for close family members, which develops into care for a whole tribe, and then a whole nation, a whole race, and finally all humanity. It's a hopeful progression Singer charts, and it even leads, eventually, to caring for animals and coral reefs and forests.

Singer imagines that our mirror neurons, our theory of mind, and our biological altruism have set us up for a future filled with empathy—an expanding circle whose momentum predates and outlasts the selfishness of our consumer culture.

ONCE A MONTH there's a grazing half-connection. Kenny began taking his mother out on walks around the neighbourhood. A couple blocks from the care centre there were quiet, residential streets. She was no longer interested in the trees and flowers that all her life had been objects of fascination (when we cleaned out her bedroom I found stacks of pressed flowers, including two perfectly preserved four-leaf clovers). Now she moved, head down, wrapped in scarves, asking where her husband was, where Kenny was—"right here, Omma." Conversations were impossible, with senseless answers offered to unasked questions, utterances made of two separate thoughts glue-gunned together. In the absence of conversation, Kenny held his mother's hand. And one day, as they walked hand in hand, circling a block and going nowhere, Kenny absent-mindedly sang the first line of one of those Patti Kim songs she used to play on YouTube. (The new facility had no computer, so it'd been weeks since she'd been able to hear them.) As though someone pressed Play at the back of her head, Omma looked up and sang out loud to the neighbourhood: "사랑할수록 깊어가는 슬픔에 . . ." *The deeper my love gets, the deeper my sorrow gets . . .*

She did not stop, either. She knew the whole song. She did not know where she was, or the names of her grandchildren, or why she was being kept in an institution, but she knew the song once her son began it. She sang:

당신의 눈물이 생각날 때 기억에 남아있는 꿈들이
눈을 감으면 수많은 별이 되어 어두운 밤 하늘에 흘러
　가리 . . .
When your tears come to my mind, I close my eyes,
And the dreams lingering in my memory turn into
　countless stars,
Flowing in the dark night sky . . .
내 가슴에 봄은 멀리 있지만 내 사랑 꽃이 되고 싶어라.
Although spring is far away in my heart, my love aspires
　to be a flower.

LATE IN THE summer of 2019 the family's "preferred facility," the one that seemed best suited to Omma's needs, announced that it had a space for her. So, she was moved again. Kenny had by then spent months working through bureaucratic sludge to make this happen; a paper mix-up had assigned his mother to the wrong health authority, and they, in turn, nearly shipped her to an institution in another town.

At the new facility we walked past a lovely living area, complete with library, fish tank, and cages of tropical birds, where patients with lower needs could watch TV and chat in side-by-side wheelchairs. We kept walking. Past all that, an elevator took us upstairs to the Special Care Unit where Omma would live behind another set of code-locked doors. While Kenny did an intake interview with one of the SCU nurses, I walked Omma up and down the horseshoe hallway. I took her onto a small patio where the staff had planted green beans, cabbages, and lettuce in wooden boxes, but I couldn't get her interested in vegetables; Omma insisted that we had to keep moving, had to be somewhere else. She led me by the hand into a dead end, frowned, led me away and back again, only to find the same dead end, a ridiculous certainty confronting an anything-goes mind. We attacked the dead end a third time before I had the courage to take charge and direct her steps. Through this back-and-forthing I burned minutes waiting for Kenny to finish with the nurse. We continued our meaningless promenade and I nodded at other residents as though we were all taking a turn on some sunny boardwalk. Guiltily, I handed Omma back to Kenny at the earliest chance, ashamed of my own uselessness.

Back at our condo, after we'd left her there in the care of more professional strangers, Kenny slowly took off his shoes and said, "There are these bits of hope I didn't even know I was hanging on to. I mean, some part of me must have been hoping this whole time that things would get better if we could just get her into the right care home. I was so focused on that. And now she's there, in our *preferred facility"*—he made scare quotes in an angry little gesture as though the phrase were mocking him—"she's there and she's still sick and nothing makes it better."

Days passed, weeks. Nurses would call when Omma fell, or if she accused other residents of stealing her husband, or refused to shower, or shouted for her father, her teacher, her anybody. And Kenny would visit, again and again. He got in the habit of sneaking in, would try to see how his mother behaved with no family around. One day he stood in the doorway and watched while a volunteer played old songs on a battered upright piano. His mother was standing by the pianist, smiling and singing along to "Beautiful Brown Eyes" with the sly confidence of a lounge singer. He waited in the doorway, unsure whether to break the spell. Waiting, too, to learn which songs his mother knew.

THE GOALS OF care are so far removed from the goals of our everyday consumer culture that the one looks foreign and bizarre when you spend too much time with the other. Caring largely consists of showing up, of cutting into your life and handing over a piece, of emotional labour and settling and tamping down selfishness. Consumer culture encourages none of that and, instead, holds up a single gleaming goal for us to run toward: Happiness. The point of life, every advertisement insists, is to be happy. To win a happy day. We're offered sex appeal, or a picture-perfect family, or authority at work, or a blissful afternoon at the beach. And each fantasy is, in the moment, a *demanding* happiness that takes up the screen, a shiny loudmouth that holds no room for pain or anguish, no room for broken things that can't find a happiness of their own. No room for the weird paradoxes and hidden meanings that other experiences create. Caring for the ill wraps you in those ironies and reversals: you laugh at the wrong time, you cry over dinner. Consumerism is a simple relief by comparison, with its flat and clean-edged feelings.

Actual happiness is, of course, never exactly what you get. While we do grow happier when we can purchase our basic needs, we experience what sociologists call "declining hedonic return" the richer our culture becomes.[158] It gets harder and harder to buy our way into a good time. And so advertisers must up their game, must offer a shifting *promise* of happiness, something to tease us forward, day by day, into just one more purchase. Meanwhile, all other concerns start to feel like mistakes, like interruptions of that single pursuit. The happiness of consumer culture becomes like a well-funded lobbyist who tries to blot out all other concerns.

But, for those of us acclimatized to the bleached air of hospitals, those of us (and there are more every day) who know what it is to take hope in a mother's ability to walk around the block, happiness is not just a foreign country, it is a lesser story. Charles de Gaulle reportedly said that happy people are idiots and I think I know now what he meant: not just that happy people are merry and distracted, but that each time any of us takes refuge in a happy moment, a happy day, we are willfully blinding ourselves to larger realities. To be always happy would be to hole yourself up in a single corner of life. To be always happy would be a kind of suicide.

These days, my husband's happiness is like a hummingbird at the feeder. I drop everything to see it. These accidents of happiness after so much hardness are little miracles and I don't deny that it feels, then, like happiness must be the only point of life. It feels so, seems so. But life is not one story, it's a havoc of narratives—and real happiness is precious precisely because it bobs only a moment atop that whirl of darker matter.

AFTER WE MOVED Omma that fourth time, she began singing the old Korean songs less and less. It was as though each move shook another something loose, or perhaps it was merely the inevitable progression of her dementia, lurching downward in stages. There were a few songs that remained, anyhow, children's melodies that she had, decades earlier, sung to Kenny.

She held Kenny's hand less fervently when we visited; sometimes she would even blink as though to say, "What are *you* doing here?" It became easier to slip away behind the code-locked doors and this ease was, in a way, painful too. She decided an older gentleman, another resident, was her father, or sometimes her teacher, and she clung to him instead, driving the confused man to a state of high anxiety.

One day Kenny took her on a walk outside and, as they made their way past little houses with clean little gardens, he tried to talk to her and failed and tried to talk some more and failed some more. She answered questions that had not been asked, or combined three thoughts into a sentence so that her words became riddles. They stopped talking. And then Kenny whistled the first few bars of "You Are My Sunshine." Suddenly Omma lit up, beamed, sang to the whole street:

You are my sunshine, my only sunshine!
You make me happy when skies are grey!

Kenny, delighted, began singing along . . .

You'll never know, dear, how much I love you.

But there his voice caught and he choked, realizing suddenly what every mother knows. He'd been working years now on her behalf, woke every morning worrying, regularly wept, forced himself to be where and how she needed him to be. And she knew nothing about the care being offered. There is a selfless attention that only a caregiver knows, an attention that is not shared or reciprocated, or even acknowledged.

They walked and she sang again, happy, oblivious, charmed by her own ability to recall the words. When Omma finished her second run-through (*Please don't take my sunshine away* . . .), she laughed, clapped her hands, enjoying the applause for her performance. And then she asked to go home.

A GENERATION OF millennials, raised to chase the ease and transactional pleasures of consumerism, will learn what it means to give and get nothing back. More people than ever will move beyond a this-for-that dream and toward one-way giving instead: giving of time and energy and heartache to feeble and vulnerable—and, by then, often infuriating—elders who, as they bend toward a medically prolonged chaos, will spit and scream instead of saying thank you. Meanwhile, lowering birth rates mean youths of the future will be outnumbered by those they care for.

We're entering a culture of caring. And people like Kenny and me, who have no children, can only hope that we too will be attended to in our turn. But we cannot know how, or why, that care will come about.

I'll make this pitch, though, to my future caregiver: it's more of a bargain than it seems. Caring for another, particularly one who cannot give back, draws us into an enormous, lasting network of human concern. What do we get for our trouble? We get the chance to contribute, for once; to give in a world that encourages such endless taking. Our true inheritance waits not in some oil field or trust fund, but in our elemental bonds. And it's through our supposed sacrifices that we manage to finally account for our own lives.

AS I WROTE the above, Kenny's mother of course grew worse. Her frontal lobe, the seat of her reason and emotional control, failed far faster than other parts of her brain, and she began hitting her caretakers. She was taken back to the psych ward at Mount Saint Joseph where she kicked one of the nurses, was held down by a team, and injected with something to make her woozy. We sat on the edge of her hospital bed, in Emergency, and listened to the kindly psychiatrist, the same one who'd handled her first intake all those many months ago. We were cordoned off in Bed #2, but there were a dozen other beds in the room, each one circled with a veil of blue curtain. And as I made my rounds, fetching sandwiches or coffees or waters, I heard bits of conversation behind each curtain. There was an elderly man apparently overdosing, another with blood filling his chest cavity, a woman with dementia even worse than Omma's. A series of private emergencies and—for the lucky ones—little circles of people around each patient, people murmuring, listening, consoling. I found myself eavesdropping at those curtains, breaching sacred privacies, and wondering just how much of this beaten-down care goes unadvertised, unacknowledged, in our shiny, happy world.

We must all be babies, in the end. And the world sings: *You'll never know, dear.*

KENNY'S MOTHER WAS still in the psych ward when her birthday rolled around. But what gift do you buy a woman who cannot understand where she is, let alone the value of a cashmere sweater or a hardback novel? Kenny bought her a glossy apple tart, which she looked at briefly before turning away. She couldn't seem to recognize that this might be something she wanted. He brought a little to her lips and she enjoyed the morsel, but then immediately lost interest again. The dessert remained uneaten, a shining cipher. The instinct to want something seemed to have drained away.

Weeks later, COVID-19 reached our part of the world. It shuttered the shops and restaurants, silenced the beaches and streets, swept us into quarantines. And it caused the care homes to ban all visitations. We could not know whether Omma would recognize her family at all by the time the pandemic had passed. There was nothing to do but hope that, somehow, enough had already been done. But what would "enough" even mean?

Shortly before the doors were locked against us, Kenny was sitting by his mother and she suddenly lit up, straightened in her chair. "Kenny," she said, "let's go buy some apples."

"Okay, Omma. Let's go buy some apples."

But they didn't head out to the shop, of course, they only sat and held hands. Shopping was a too-simple story from another, simpler life that barely made sense anymore.

10

ORANGE AND BLUE

LIFE IS NOT a story. It's many.

To give our lives some semblance of meaning or purpose we impose narratives every day, every hour. We name the princes and villains. We tell ourselves why, and for what reason. But to draw always on the same story is to impose a kind of poverty, an insupportable narrowing of experience and imagination. When, in the twentieth century, many of us narrowed things down to the single story of consumption we unwittingly narrowed our view of the natural world, too—the Earth became just one more thing to consume.

In exchange, we were promised a celebration of the individual, that this story of ours would make us into happy heroes. A greedy inertia implied that the more we gathered and grasped, the more our heroics would be revealed. And the heroic tale *was* working—for a while. But the long-term reality was bleaker, stingier. Whole quadrants of experience were blotted out as attention siphoned toward the monolithic consumer narrative.

This book chronicles a time when I, anxious in that half-blind state, twisted around and looked for the missing stories. Whole generations are doing likewise. We supposed they'd be waiting for us, fully formed. But when I turned from the wreckage of consumer culture toward Craft, toward the Sublime, toward Care, I found only the vaguest representations. Static in the air.

These other stories were using a different language than the mono-myth of our time. Where consumer culture offers something finished, Craft offers something coming into being; where consumer culture offers something you own, the Sublime offers something beyond your grasp; and where consumer culture offers satisfaction, Care invites sacrifice and devotion. All these alternatives turn our attention away from the untenable answer we were offered before. In its place, we get lived experience, Aristotle's eudaimonia, a humble, reverential rhythm.

What does it mean to do good work? Where do you belong in an indifferent universe? Can we support the most vulnerable among us? Ongoing questions like these could replace our closed tale of consumerism. If they seem too vague at first, that's because consumerism has done such an excellent job of belittling them. "Craft," in our culture, became an artisanal cup of coffee; "the Sublime" became a *Star Wars* movie; and "Care" became a beauty product. We've grown used to thinking of other stories as non-essential, as luxuries.

In fact, they are elemental. Craft is how we survived for millennia. The Sublime shaped our sense of being long before the rise of consumer culture. And Care is perhaps our single most important survival tactic. Such supposedly inessential stories are really the base ingredients of human life. And bringing them into focus would get us partway to the fix we've been waiting for. Whether we take up these alternatives by choice, or only in a desperate reaction to climate disasters, is less certain.

ON THE PRETTY hill of garbage where my research began, I looked cynically at the orange and blue flowers growing in a skin of dirt. I thought at first they were only a way to cover up the trash, a way to try to forget all the waste beneath.

I see those flowers differently now. They are a bit of covering up, yes, but not only that. They're also a hint, a reminder, that humans keep insisting on grace and new chances.

Our future is nothing more and nothing less than a synthesis of our past. Our own story-lives are growing straight up and out from a troubled yesterday, like flowers on the flank of a landfill. And the stories we embrace, these new—and very old—ways of measuring a life, will not always just shiver in the air as I've been imagining, unresolved, barely legible. They are becoming tactile things, rooted and plainly alive. They are insistent and green, and just beginning to open.

NOTES

1.   The World Bank, "Global Waste on Pace to Triple by 2100,"
      World Bank, October 30, 2013, http://datatopics.worldbank.org
      /what-a-waste/.
2.   "UN Report: Time to Seize Opportunity, Tackle Challenge of
      E-Waste," January 24, 2019, https://www.unenvironment.org
      /news-and-stories/press-release/un-report-time-seize
      -opportunity-tackle-challenge-e-waste.
3.   Megan Garber, "The Trash We've Left on the Moon," *The Atlantic*,
      December 19, 2012, https://www.theatlantic.com/technology
      /archive/2012/12/the-trash-weve-left-on-the-moon/266465/.
4.   NASA, "Space Debris and Human Spacecraft," September 26,
      2013, https://www.nasa.gov/mission_pages/station/news
      /orbital_debris.html.
5.   City of Vancouver, "2019 Annual Report for the Vancouver
      Landfill," March 31, 2020, https://vancouver.ca/files/cov/2019
      -vancouver-landfill-annual-report.pdf.
6.   Hillary Hoffower, "Meet the Average American Millennial,"
      Business Insider, February 27, 2020, https://www.businessinsider
      .com/average-american-millennial-net-worth-student-loan
      -debt-savings-habits-2019-6#and-the-typical-millennial-has
      -less-than-5000-in-their-savings-account-3.
7.   Kim Parker and Ruth Igielnik, "On the Cusp of Adulthood and
      Facing an Uncertain Future," Pew Research Center, May 14, 2020,
      https://www.pewsocialtrends.org/essay/on-the-cusp-of
      -adulthood-and-facing-an-uncertain-future-what-we-know
      -about-gen-z-so-far/.

8. Lenny Bernstein, "U.S. Life Expectancy Declines Again, a Dismal Trend Not Seen Since World War One," *Washington Post*, November 28, 2018, https://www.washingtonpost.com /national/health-science/us-life-expectancy-declines-again-a -dismal-trend-not-seen-since-world-war-i/2018/11/28/ae58bc8c -f28c-11e8-bc79-68604ed88993_story.html.

9. Harriet Pike, "Life Expectancy in England and Wales Has Fallen by Six Months," *BMJ* 364 (March 11, 2019), 1123.

10. This is partly due to the fact that living solo has become vastly more common among today's young than in previous genera- tions—a change that has large material consequences since each solo living arrangement involves furniture, appliances, and space that would otherwise be shared.

11. UN Environment, "Our Planet is Drowning in Plastic Pollution," accessed October 14, 2019, https://www.unenvironment.org /interactive/beat-plastic-pollution/.

12. Homi Kharas, "The Unprecedented Expansion of the Global Middle Class: An Update," Global Economy and Development at Brookings, February 2017.

13. William Rees, "Memo from a Climate Crisis Realist," *The Tyee*, November 12, 2019, https://thetyee.ca/Analysis/2019/11/12 /Climate-Crisis-Realist-Memo/.

14. Frank Tang, "China's Globalisation Pioneer Says It Is Now Time to Look Closer to Home amid US Decoupling Moves," *South China Morning Post*, June 8, 2020, https://www.scmp.com /economy/china-economy/article/3088060/chinas -globalisation-pioneer-says-it-now-time-look-closer.

15. The World Bank, "CO_2 Emissions (metric tons per capita)," https://data.worldbank.org/indicator/EN.ATM.CO2E.PC?end= 2014&start=1960&view=chart.

16. Author interview with Dorrik Stow, Professor of Petroleum Geoscience, Heriot-Watt University, June 11, 2019.

17. BP, "Statistical Review of World Energy: 2020," 14–15, https:// www.bp.com/content/dam/bp/business-sites/en/global /corporate/pdfs/energy-economics/statistical-review/bp-stats -review-2020-full-report.pdf.

18. Nadia Drake, "Our Nights Are Getting Brighter and Earth Is Paying the Price," *National Geographic*, April 3, 2019, https://www.nationalgeographic.com/science/2019/04/nights-are-getting-brighter-earth-paying-the-price-light-pollution-dark-skies/.

19. Mike Carlowicz, "Summer Blooms in the Baltic and Barents," NASA, https://earthobservatory.nasa.gov/images/92462/summer-blooms-in-the-baltic-and-barents.

20. Scottie Andrew, "A Heat Wave in Antarctica Melted 20% of an Island's Snow in 9 Days," CNN.com, February 24, 2020, https://www.cnn.com/2020/02/24/world/antarctica-heat-wave-melt-february-trnd/index.html.

21. Scott A. Kulp and Benjamin H. Strauss, "New Elevation Data Triple Estimates of Global Vulnerability to Sea-level Rise and Coastal Flooding," *Nature Communications* 10 (2019), 4844.

22. Jamie Tarabay, "Why These Australia Fires Are Like Nothing We've Seen Before," *The New York Times*, January 21, 2020, https://www.nytimes.com/2020/01/21/world/australia/fires-size-climate.html.

23. Damien Cave, "The End of Australia as We Know It," *The New York Times*, February 15, 2020, https://www.nytimes.com/2020/02/15/world/australia/fires-climate-change.html.

24. Damien Cave, "The Fires Are Out, But Australia's Climate Disasters Aren't Over," *The New York Times*, February 23, 2020, https://www.nytimes.com/2020/02/23/world/australia/climate-change-extremes.html.

25. "World is 'On Notice' as Major UN Report Shows One Million Species Face Extinction," May 6, 2019, https://news.un.org/en/story/2019/05/1037941.

26. Elizabeth Pennisi, "Three Billion North American Birds Have Vanished Since 1970, Surveys Show," *Science*, September 19, 2019, https://www.sciencemag.org/news/2019/09/three-billion-north-american-birds-have-vanished-1970-surveys-show.

27. Donella H. Meadows, Dennis L. Meadows, Jørgen Randers, and William W. Behrens III, *The Limits to Growth* (New York: Universe Books, 1972), 23.

28. Ibid., 157.

29. Ibid., 170.

30. Wilfred Beckerman, *Two Cheers for the Affluent Society* (New York: Saint Martin's Press, 1974), 91–2.

31. Matthew Simmons, "Revisiting The Limits to Growth: Could the Club of Rome Have Been Correct, After All?" September 29, 2000, https://www.estudiomc.es/documentos/revisiting-the-limits-to-growth.pdf.

32. This sort of measurement can offer a radically different take on how each country is faring. One, called the Genuine Progress Indicator, which measures twenty-four quality-of-life indices, found the United States has been in decline since 1973.

33. Fiona Harvey, "Britons Want Quality of Life Indicators to Take Priority Over Economy," *The Guardian,* May 10, 2020, https://www.theguardian.com/society/2020/may/10/britons-want-quality-of-life-indicators-priority-over-economy-coronavirus.

34. NASA, "Global Climate Change: Vital Signs of the Planet," November 2020, https://climate.nasa.gov/vital-signs/carbon-dioxide/.

35. Simon Kuznets, *The National Income 1929–1932*, National Bureau of Economic Research, 1934.

36. Simon Kuznets, "How to Judge Quality," *New Republic*, October 20, 1962.

37. World Health Organization, "Health Benefits Far Outweigh the Costs of Meeting Climate Change Goals," December 5, 2018, https://www.who.int/news-room/detail/05-12-2018-health-benefits-far-outweigh-the-costs-of-meeting-climate-change-goals.

38. USGRCP, "Fourth National Climate Assessment: Volume II," (2018), https://nca2018.globalchange.gov/.

39. World Meteorological Organization, "Hurricane Dorian Causes Devastation in Bahamas," September 3, 2019, https://public.wmo.int/en/media/news/hurricane-dorian-causes-devastation-bahamas.

40. Laura Payton, "Climate Change Could Cost Billions a Year by 2020," September 29, 2011, https://www.cbc.ca/news/politics/climate-change-could-cost-billions-a-year-by-2020-1.1097373.

41. Economist Intelligence Unit, "Global Economy Will Be Three Percent Smaller by 2050 Due to Lack of Climate Resilience," November 20, 2019, https://www.eiu.com/n/global-economy-will-be-3-percent-smaller-by-2050-due-to-lack-of-climate-resilience/.

42. It was Jevons who articulated in his *Theory of Political Economy* that the value of a thing derives not from the materials and labour that went into making it but, rather, from the desire of the consumer. A good has value because it is wanted. Jevons imagined a whole economic approach based on desire rather than need.

43. Remarks by UN Secretary General at Pre-COP25 Press Conference, December 1, 2019, https://www.un.org/sg/en/content/sg/press-encounter/2019-12-01/un-secretary-generals-remarks-pre-cop25-press-conference-delivered.

44. BP, "Statistical Review of World Energy: 2019," https://www.bp.com/content/dam/bp/business-sites/en/global/corporate/pdfs/energy-economics/statistical-review/bp-stats-review-2019-full-report.pdf.

45. What's more, even if a majority of energy were derived from solar panels and wind turbines tomorrow, we'd still need to confront the fact that their construction and regular replacement require huge amounts of steel, concrete, and plastic, along with copper and rare earth elements like neodymium, which are mined by an industry reliant on fossil fuels.

46. US Energy Information Administration, "International Energy Outlook 2019," https://www.eia.gov/outlooks/aeo/data/browser/#/?id=2-IEO2019&sourcekey=0.

47. Kate Raworth, "A Healthy Economy Should Be Designed to Thrive, Not Grow," TED2018, April, 2018, https://www.ted.com/talks/kate_raworth_a_healthy_economy_should_be_designed_to_thrive_not_grow?language=en.

48. Frank Trentman, *Empire of Things* (London: Penguin Books, 2016), 664.

49. Naomi Xu Elegant, "The Internet Cloud Has a Dirty Secret," *Fortune,* September 18, 2019, https://fortune.com/2019/09/18/internet-cloud-server-data-center-energy-consumption-renewable-coal/.

50. The supposedly immaterial internet does have its own carbon footprint, and it's expanding rapidly as we add a billion new users every few years. The clean-sounding "cloud" where all our data lives is, in fact, a huge fleet of hidden server farms that dump as much carbon into the atmosphere as the entire planet's aviation industry.

51. Riley DeHaan, "Distrust, Discrimination, Trade Deficits," *Stanford Daily*, December 10, 2019, https://www.stanforddaily .com/2019/12/10/distrust-discrimination-trade-deficits-abhijit -banerjee-speaks-on-human-element-of-economics/.

52. James Ellsmoor, "New Zealand Ditches GDP for Happiness and Wellbeing," *Forbes*, July 11, 2019, https://www.forbes.com/sites /jamesellsmoor/2019/07/11/new-zealand-ditches-gdp-for -happiness-and-wellbeing/#5ba08f071942.

53. "World Population Projected to Reach 9.8 Billion in 2050 and 11.2 Billion in 2100," June 21, 2017, United Nations Department of Economic and Social Affairs, https://www.un.org/development /desa/en/news/population/world-population-prospects-2017 .html.

54. Darrel Bricker and John Ibbitson, "What Goes Up: Are Predictions of a Population Crisis Wrong?" *The Guardian*, January 27, 2019, https://www.theguardian.com/world/2019 /jan/27/what-goes-up-population-crisis-wrong-fertility-rates -decline.

55. Interview with Daniel Lieberman.

56. The advantage holds true today; we each have millions of eccrine sweat glands.

57. Fred H. Previc, *The Dopaminergic Mind in Human Evolution and History* (Cambridge: Cambridge University Press, 2009), 108–14.

58. This also explains why Parkinson's patients, whose dopamine levels are depleted, can experience reduced sweating and trouble with body heat regulation.

59. Alana Semuels, "We are all Accumulating Mountains of Things," *The Atlantic*, August 21, 2018, https://www.theatlantic.com /technology/archive/2018/08/online-shopping-and-accumulation -of-junk/567985/.

60. Author interview with Kent Berridge.
61. Stephen Lambert (producer) and Adam Curtis (director), *The Century of the Self* [motion picture] (England: BBC, 2002).
62. Ibid.
63. Larry Tye, *The Father of Spin* (New York: Henry Holt and Co., 1998), 28–9.
64. Andrew Bennett and Ann O'Reilly, *Consumed* (New York: Palgrave Macmillan, 2010), 6.
65. Tim Wu, *The Attention Merchants* (New York: Knopf, 2016), 56–7.
66. Paul M. Mazur, *American Prosperity: Its Causes and Consequences* (New York: The Viking Press, 1928), 24–5.
67. He came by the analogy honestly: in 1920, a decade before he was president of the United States, Herbert Hoover was President of the Federation of American Engineering Societies.
68. Niall Ferguson, *Civilization* (New York: Penguin, 2011), 200.
69. Lewis Mumford, *Technics and Civilization* (Chicago: University of Chicago Press, 1934), 273–4.
70. Larry Tye, *The Father of Spin* (New York: Henry Holt and Co., 1998), 38.
71. Ibid., 40.
72. Ruth Schwartz Cowan, *More Work for Mother* (New York: Basic Books, 1983).
73. Kenneth E. Hagin, *New Thresholds of Faith* (Tulsa: Faith Library Publications, 1972), 54–55.
74. Daniel Bell, *The End of Ideology*, (Cambridge: Harvard University Press, 2001), 399–400.
75. Exploiting status anxiety was an early specialty of ad men. And the fantasy of upward class mobility in "the land of opportunity" remains powerful today, though America actually offers less mobility than many other wealthy countries. An American born into a family in the bottom fifth of earners has only a 7.8 percent chance of ending up in the top fifth, but Americans consistently overestimate their ability to achieve such a leap.
76. William James, *The Principals of Psychology* (New York City: Henry Holt and Co., 1890), 401.
77. Ibid., 292.

78. Ibid., 294.
79. Procter & Gamble, "The Talk Ad," August 4, 2017, https://www
.washingtonpost.com/video/business/procter-and-gamble-the
-talk-ad/2017/08/04/52345b76-7940-11e7-8c17-533c52b2f014
_video.html.
80. Tim Nudd, "Audi's Feminist Super Bowl Ad Is a Father Daughter
Tale About Equal Pay," *Adweek,* February 1, 2017, https://www
.adweek.com/brand-marketing/audis-feminist-super-bowl-ad
-is-a-father-daughter-tale-about-equal-pay/.
81. Tim Nudd, "Apple Enlists Carl Sagan for Beautiful Tribute to
Earth After US Exit from Paris Accord," *Adweek,* June 8, 2017,
https://www.adweek.com/creativity/apple-enlists-carl-sagan
-for-beautiful-tribute-to-earth-after-u-s-exit-from-paris-accord/.
82. Daniel D'Addario, "Why the Kendall Jenner Pepsi Ad Was Such
a Glaring Misstep," *Time,* April 5, 2017, https://time.com
/4726500/pepsi-ad-kendall-jenner/.
83. Tom Peters, "The Brand Called You," *Fast Company*, August 31,
1997.
84. "Children Would Rather Become Popstars Than Teachers and
Lawyers," *The Telegraph*, October 1, 2009, https://www.telegraph
.co.uk/education/educationnews/6250626/Children-would
-rather-become-popstars-than-teachers-or-lawyers.html.
85. Yelena Dzhanova, "Forget Law School, These Kids Want to Be a
YouTube Star," CNBC, August 3, 2019, https://www.cnbc.com
/2019/08/02/forget-law-school-these-kids-want-to-be-a-youtube
-star.html.
86. "About," InfluencerMarketingHub, https://influencermarketing
hub.com/influencer-marketing-agencies/obviously/.
87. Federal Reserve Bank of New York, *Quarterly Report on
Household Debt and Credit*, May 2021, https://www.newyorkfed
.org/medialibrary/interactives/householdcredit/data/pdf
/hhdc_2021q1.pdf.
88. Yuval Noah Harari, *21 Lessons for the 21st Century* (Toronto:
Signal, 2018), 291.
89. Michael Kwet, "In Stores, Secret Bluetooth Surveillance Tracks
Your Every Move," *The New York Times,* June 14, 2019, https://

www.nytimes.com/interactive/2019/06/14/opinion
/bluetooth-wireless-tracking-privacy.html.

90. Tim Wu, *The Attention Merchants* (New York: Knopf, 2016), 296.

91. Naomi Klein, *On Fire* (Toronto: Knopf, 2019), 245.

92. In Britain, a similar Keep Britain Tidy campaign was launched; chaired by the managing director of Shell-Mex and BP Ltd., the joint petroleum marketing venture, Keep Britain Tidy exhorted citizens to stop abandoning cars in the countryside.

93. Frank Trentmann, *Empire of Things* (London: Penguin Books, 2016), 675.

94. Larry Tye, *The Father of Spin* (New York: Henry Holt and Co., 1998), 46.

95. Ibid., 47.

96. Author interview with Dr. Edith Hall, September 11, 2019.

97. Aristotle, *Nicomachean Ethics,* trans. J. A. K. Thomson (London: Penguin Books, 1953), 16.

98. E. L. Deci and R. M. Ryan, "Hedonia, Eudaimonia, and Well-being: An Introduction," *Journal of Happiness Studies* 9, no. 1 (2008), 1–11.

99. Aristotle, *Nicomachean Ethics*, trans. J. A. K. Thomson (London: Penguin Books, 1953), 16.

100. Alexia Fernández Campbell, "CEOs Made 287 Times More Money Last Year Than Their Workers Did," *Vox*, June 26, 2019, https://www.vox.com/policy-and-politics/2019/6/26/18744304/ceo-pay-ratio-disclosure-2018.

101. Katherine Schaeffer, "Six Facts About Economic Inequality in the U.S.," Pew Research Center, February 7, 2020, https://www.pewresearch.org/fact-tank/2020/02/07/6-facts-about-economic-inequality-in-the-u-s/.

102. Dean Baker, "This Is What Minimum Wage Would Be If It Kept Pace with Productivity," Center for Economic and Policy Research, January 21, 2020, https://cepr.net/this-is-what-minimum-wage-would-be-if-it-kept-pace-with-productivity/.

103. Francis Fukuyama, "The End of History?" *The National Interest* 16 (Summer 1989), 3–18.

104. James Atlas, "What is Fukuyama Saying? And to Whom is He Saying it?" *The New York Times*, October 22, 1989.

105. Ibid.

106. Karl Marx, *The Political Writings* (London: Verso, 2019), 289.

107. PWC, "How Will Automation Impact Jobs?" https://www.pwc
.co.uk/automation.

108. James Manyika et al., "Jobs Lost, Jobs Gained," McKinsey Global
Institute, November 28, 2017, https://www.mckinsey.com/featured
-insights/future-of-work/jobs-lost-jobs-gained-what-the-future-of
-work-will-mean-for-jobs-skills-and-wages.

109. Ben Dobbin, "Kodak Chairman Struggles to Develop Efficiency,"
Los Angeles Times, December 6, 1994, https://www.latimes.com
/archives/la-xpm-1994-12-06-fi-5505-story.html.

110. Avery Hartmans, "Instagram Is Celebrating Its Tenth Birthday,"
Business Insider, October 6, 2020, https://www.businessinsider
.com/instagram-first-13-employees-full-list-2020-4.

111. "We have been expressly evolved by nature," wrote John
Maynard Keynes, "with all our impulses and deepest instincts—
for the purpose of solving the economic problem. If the economic problem is solved, mankind will be deprived of its
traditional purpose. . . . I think with dread of the readjustment
of the habits and instincts of the ordinary man, bred into him
for countless generations, which he may be asked to discard
within a few decades." Some of us now live in the shade of
Keynes's dread. While he could not anticipate the ecological
fallout that a materialist paradise would produce, he still understood that the twentieth century was not merely leading up to
some everlasting pleasure cruise but to a dilemma about the
basic purpose of our lives.

112. The World Bank, "Labour Force Participation Rate," September
20, 2020, https://data.worldbank.org/indicator/SL.TLF.CACT.ZS.

113. E. F. Schumacher, *Small is Beautiful* (London: Vintage, 1993), 40.

114. Mihaly Csikszentmihalyi, *Flow: The Psychology of Optimal
Experience* (New York: Harper Perennial Modern Classics,
2007), 3.

115. Edward McEwen et al., "Early Bow Design and Construction,"
Scientific American, June 1991.

116. Ibid.

117. Allan Hall, "Ikea buys 83,000 Acre Forest in Romania to Make Furniture," *The Times*, July 1, 2015, https://www.thetimes.co.uk /article/ikea-buys-83000-acre-forest-in-romania-to-make -furniture-7g6bgk9fphj.
118. Email to author from Parks Canada, January 17, 2019.
119. Samuel Taylor Coleridge, "France: An Ode," *The Complete Poetical Works of Samuel Taylor Coleridge* (Oxford: Clarendon Press, 1912), 243.
120. Samuel Taylor Coleridge, "Letter to Sara Hutchinson 6th August 1802," in *Collected Letters of Samuel Taylor Coleridge*, ed. Earl Leslie Griggs (Oxford: Oxford University Press, 2000/1802), 841.
121. Donovan Webster, "Inside the Volcano," in *The Best American Science and Nature Writing 2001*, ed. Edward O. Wilson (Boston: Houghton Mifflin, 2001), 253–4.
122. John Bellamy Foster, "Marx's Theory of Metabolic Rift," *American Journal of Sociology* 105, no. 2 (September 1999), 366–405.
123. "Children Spend Only Half As Much Time Playing Outside as Their Parents Did," *The Guardian*, July 27, 2016, https://www .theguardian.com/environment/2016/jul/27/children-spend -only-half-the-time-playing-outside-as-their-parents-did.
124. United States Environmental Protection Agency, "Indoor Air Quality," https://www.epa.gov/report-environment/indoor-air -quality#note1.
125. Richard Louv, *The Nature Principle* (New York: Algonquin Books of Chapel Hill, 2012), 11.
126. Ibid., 105–177.
127. Alan Weisman, "Earth Without People," *Discover*, February 5, 2005.
128. James Gallagher, "More Than Half Your Body Is Not Human," BBC News, April 10, 2018, http://www.bbc.com/news/health -43674270.
129. Thomas Burnet, *The Sacred Theory of the Earth* (Glasgow: R. Urie, 1753), 65.
130. Ibid., 65.
131. Gilbert Burnet, *Some Letters Containing an Account of what seemed Most Remarkable in travelling through Switzerland, Italy,*

and some parts of Germany in the years 1685 and 1686 (London: J. Lacy, 1724), 15.

132. David W. Krueger, "The Use of Money as an Action Symptom," in *I Shop, Therefore I Am: Compulsive Buying and the Search for Self*, ed. April Lane Benson (Toronto: Rowman and Littlefield, 2004), 291.

133. Linda Marie Brooks, *The Menace of the Sublime to the Individual Self* (New York: Edwin Mellen Press, 1995), 17.

134. José María Heredia, *Torrente Prodigioso: A Cuban Poet at Niagara Falls*, ed. and trans. Keith Ellis (Toronto: Lugus, 1997), 21.

135. Albert Einstein, *Ideas and Opinions* (New York: Crown Publishers, 1954), 11.

136. Ibid.

137. Iian I. Goldberg et al., "When the Brain Loses Its Self," *Neuron* 50 (April 20, 2006), 329–339.

138. Alzheimer's Disease International, "Dementia Statistics," https://www.alz.co.uk/research/statistics.

139. World Health Organization, "Dementia," September 21, 2020, http://www.who.int/news-room/fact-sheets/detail/dementia.

140. United Nations, Department of Economic and Social Affairs, "World Population Prospects 2019," https://population.un.org/wpp/Publications/Files/WPP2019_Highlights.pdf.

141. US Department of Health and Human Services, Health Resources and Services Administration, Bureau of Health Work, National Center for Health Workforce Analysis, "National and Regional Projections of Supply and Demand for Geriatricians: 2013–2025," April 2017, https://bhw.hrsa.gov/sites/default/files/bhw/health-workforce-analysis/research/projections/GeriatricsReport51817.pdf.

142. Ibid.

143. Alzheimer's Disease International, "Dementia Statistics," https://www.alz.co.uk/research/statistics.

144. US Department of Commerce, "Population Estimates," April 17, 1969, https://www.census.gov/prod/1/pop/p25-420.pdf.

145. Alexandre Tanzi and Shelly Hagan, "Half of Americans Are Now Over the Age of 38," *Bloomberg*, June 19, 2019, https://www.bloomberg.com/news/articles/2019-06-20/half-of-americans-are-now-over-the-age-of-38-census-data-show.

146. Jane Reister Conrad, "Granny Dumping: The Hospital's Duty of Care to Patients Who Have Nowhere to Go," *Yale Law & Policy Review* 10, no. 2 (1992), 463–87.
147. "Granny Dumping by the Thousands," *The New York Times*, March 29, 1992.
148. Frans de Waal, *Our Inner Ape,* (New York: Riverhead Books, 2006), 170.
149. Frans de Waal, *Bonobo: The Forgotten Ape* (Berkeley: University of California Press, 1997), 157.
150. Susan Nesser, "Zoo Story," *Milwaukee Magazine,* August 2007.
151. Stephen Jay Gould, *Ever Since Darwin* (Harmondsworth, UK: Penguin, 1980), 261.
152. Sandra Blakeslee, "Cells That Read Minds," *The New York Times,* January 10, 2006.
153. Frans de Waal, *Our Inner Ape* (New York: Riverhead Books, 2006), 177.
154. Laura Geggel, "Yawning Not Contagious for Children with Autism," *Scientific American,* September 23, 2013, https://www.scientificamerican.com/article/yawning-not-contagious-for-children-with-autism/.
155. Frans de Waal, *The Age of Empathy* (New York: Three Rivers Press, 2009), 49.
156. Frans de Waal, *Our Inner Ape* (New York: Riverhead Books, 2006), 174.
157. Peter Singer, *The Expanding Circle* (Princeton: Princeton University Press, 1981/2011).
158. Robert E. Lane, *The Loss of Happiness in Market Democracies* (New Haven: Yale University Press, 2000), 61.

ACKNOWLEDGEMENTS

This book was completed during the COVID-19 pandemic. Kindness seems to cost more during this gruelling period; so, thanking those who were kind enough to help me out (or drag me along) feels especially important.

My thanks to the dozens of experts who told me about their work, and especially to: Lynn Belanger, Kent Berridge, Don Gardner, Edith Hall, Daniel Lieberman, Matthew Pelowski, Jørgen Randers, and Dorrik Stow.

Thanks to Eugene Kim and Maki Yi for their careful translations.

Before the pandemic struck, I spent a month at the Banff Centre, and part of this book was written there. My thanks to all the faculty and participants—it was a charmed and inspiring time.

For writerly camaraderie, thanks to my dear Camp friends: Anne Casselman, Arno Kopecky, and James MacKinnon.

I'm deeply indebted to my agents, Anne McDermid and Suzanne Brandreth, who shepherd things along with such care and wisdom.

Ward Hawkes and Martha Kanya-Forstner are both extraordinary editors whose kind counsel and level heads made this book possible. Thank you, both, for your belief in this book and for your profound patience.

There were times, writing these pages, when I felt less like an author and more like a thief, stealing ideas from my husband, Kenny Park. The best parts of this book are his.

I acknowledge the support of the Canada Council for the Arts.

 Canada Council   Conseil des arts
for the Arts   du Canada

MICHAEL HARRIS is the bestselling author of *The End of Absence* and *Solitude*. A recipient of the Governor General's Literary Award, he is also a faculty member in the Literary Journalism program at the Banff Centre and the writer of the award-winning podcast *Command Line Heroes*. He lives with his husband in Vancouver.

MichaelJohnHarris.com
@VancouverHarris

A NOTE ABOUT THE TYPE

The text of *All We Want* has been set in Kepler, a contemporary Adobe Originals typeface designed by Robert Slimbach in the tradition of classic modern 18th century serifs. Named after the German astronomer Kepler, the typeface recalls the elegant and refined typefaces popular among Renaissance printers and typesetters. While Kepler has Oldstyle proportions, calligraphic detailing lends the typeface humanistic warmth and energy.